CULTURAL REPRESENTATION IN NATIVE AMERICA

CONTEMPORARY NATIVE AMERICAN COMMUNITIES
Stepping Stones to the Seventh Generation

Acknowledging the strength and vibrancy of Native American people and nations today, this series examines life in contemporary Native American communities from the point of view of Native concerns and values. These new publications are intended to be correctives to the misconceptions that still appear in many books and in the American imagination: that Indian people largely disappeared or were assimilated after 1890. Books in the series cover topics that are of cultural and political importance to tribal peoples and that affect their possibilities for survival, in both urban and rural communities.

SERIES EDITORS:

Troy Johnson, American Indian Studies, California State University, Long Beach, Long Beach, CA 90840, trj@csulb.edu

Duane Champagne, Native Nations Law and Policy Center, 292 Haines Hall, Box 951551, University of California, Los Angeles, Los Angeles, CA 90095-1551, champagn@ucla.edu

BOOKS IN THE SERIES
1. *Inuit, Whaling, and Sustainability*, Milton M. R. Freeman, Ingmar Egede, Lyudmila Bogoslovskaya, Igor G. Krupnik, Richard A. Caulfield, and Marc G. Stevenson (1999)
2. *Contemporary Native American Political Issues*, edited by Troy Johnson (1999)
3. *Contemporary Native American Cultural Issues*, edited by Duane Champagne (1999)
4. *Modern Tribal Development: Paths to Self Sufficiency and Cultural Integrity in Indian Country*, Dean Howard Smith (2000)
5. *American Indians and the Urban Experience*, edited by Susan Lobo and Kurt Peters (2000)
6. *Medicine Ways: Disease, Health, and Survival among Native Americans*, edited by Clifford Trafzer and Diane Weiner (2000)
7. *Native American Studies in Higher Education: Models for Collaboration between Universities and Indigenous Nations*, edited by Duane Champagne and Jay Stauss (2002)
8. *Spider Woman Walks This Land: Traditional Cultural Properties and the Navajo Nation*, by Kelli Carmean (2002)
9. *Alaska Native Political Leadership and Higher Education: One University, Two Universes*, by Michael Jennings (2004)
10. *Indigenous Intellectual Property Rights: Legal Obstacles and Innovative Solutions*, edited by Mary Riley (2004)

CULTURAL REPRESENTATION IN NATIVE AMERICA

Edited by
Andrew Jolivétte

ALTAMIRA
PRESS

A Division of Rowman & Littlefield Publishers, Inc.
Lanham • New York • Toronto • Plymouth, UK

ALTAMIRA PRESS
A Division of Rowman & Littlefield Publishers, Inc.
A wholly owned subsidiary of The Rowman & Littlefield Publishing Group, Inc.
4501 Forbes Boulevard, Suite 200
Lanham, MD 20706
www.altamirapress.com

Estover Road
Plymouth PL6 7PY
United Kingdom

British Library Cataloguing in Publication Information Available

Library of Congress Cataloging-in-Publication Data

Cultural representation in Native America / edited by Andrew Jolivétte.
    p.   cm. — (Contemporary Native American communities)
    Includes bibliographical references and index.
    ISBN-13: 978-0-7591-0984-1 (cloth : alk. paper)
    ISBN-10: 0-7591-0984-2 (cloth : alk. paper)
    ISBN-13: 978-0-7591-0985-8 (pbk. : alk. paper)
    ISBN-10: 0-7591-0985-0 (pbk. : alk. paper)
    1. Indians of North America—Ethnic identity. 2. Indians of North America—
Civil rights. 3. Indians of North America—Politics and government. 4. Self-
determination, National—United States. I. Jolivétte, Andrew, 1975– . II. Series.
    E99.E85C85 2006
    305.897'073—dc22   2006003161

Printed in the United States of America

⊗ ™ The paper used in this publication meets the minimum requirements of
American National Standard for Information Sciences—Permanence of Paper for
Printed Library Materials, ANSI/NISO Z39.48-1992.

Contents

Foreword

From 1993 to 1996 I worked with the Los Angeles City/County American Indian Commission on a task force whose mandate was to end the use of American Indian words, names, and images as mascots on sports teams at all California elementary schools and high schools. This effort often involved meeting with school district administrators, school principals, and members of local Parent Teacher Associations (PTAs). On one such occasion, when scheduling a meeting before a PTA organization, the PTA president requested that an American Indian be present to whom PTA members could address specific questions in order to better understand the issues involved.

There were a number of American Indian private citizens and professionals on our task force, and so we arranged for one of them, a member of the California Bar Association and a partner in a very successful law practice, to visit a PTA meeting in session. The attorney arrived directly from a Los Angeles courtroom wearing the "traditional regalia" expected of a practicing attorney in a Los Angeles courtroom: a three-piece business suit.

Upon arrival at the PTA meeting the attorney was escorted to a seat on the speaker's platform. After some preliminary housekeeping announcements, the PTA president turned to the platform guests, turned to the PTA vice president, and in a semi-panicked voice said, "Where is *our* Indian?" The American Indian attorney rose in a dignified manner and approached the speaker's podium and said, "My name is Walter Boudrow.[1] I am from the Lakota and Pawnee Nations. Some people call me an Indian or American Indian. But I can assure you that *I am not YOUR Indian.*"[2]

Contestation! Why is it that in the twenty-first century American Indian people[3] must resort to contestation to claim their natural identity and traditional location in the world? It is with this question in mind that the authors in this book set out to address the myriad facets of Native identity, culture, lifeways, cosmology, and activism that make up the sacred space in which Native people live, work, play, and raise their families. As you read you will find that the answer is not an easy one. Whether through the portrayal of a Barbie doll or a racist mascot, the disrespect of Native women, the commodification of all things "Indian," or the rise of activism, Native People continue to be challenged in their very existence.

One can accurately say that Native People have been in a posture of contestation for space and identity since contact with European savages in the Caribbean in the 1400s.[4] Europeans traveling in the guise of explorers and conquistadores kidnapped, killed, and in other ways attacked the very existence of Native Peoples. Recovery has come slowly, but most certainly recovery has come!

The authors in this collection divide their approach to contestation into three areas: contestation and representation, contestation and politics, and contestation and mixed-race identity. As is true in all areas of Native life, however, these are best seen as a whole, not in parts. Oral history, personal narrative, and historical recollections are intrinsic necessities to the understanding of Native politics and Native identity. Native politics appear, disappear, and reappear in Native narrative, identity, and discourse. Native representation is at the heart of Native politics and Native activism. The discussion of corporate shamanism cannot be understood without an understanding of the historical context of shamanism, which is best represented in oral history and personal narrative. This, I suppose, is the short way of stating that all things Native are incorporated within the sacred circle of Native cosmology and that they must continuously be contested to insure survival and to validate authenticity.

Contestation is a necessary action. Without contestation people tend to accept their place in the world order over time. Those who have been relegated to a lesser space by a dominant society accept that position through fear of discrimination, retaliation, or lack of power. It is only through challenge that revitalization and healing come about. It is only through challenge that the dominant paradigm of cultural misrepresentation, appropriation, and identity can be destroyed and a new paradigm developed that allows the true identity and persona of the Native Person to be recognized and respected.

Much to the dismay of many governmental figures as well as private citizens, Native Americans have not died out, disappeared, or been subsumed within the dominant society. They are contesting, through different media and actions.

Dr. Troy Johnson
Chair, American Indian Studies Program
California State University, Long Beach, California

Notes

1. The name has been changed at the request of the attorney.
2. Emphasis added to capture the delivery of the speaker.
3. It is with great respect that I approach the use of words/names such as Indian, American Indian, Native American, and Native Peoples. For a cogent discussion of these terms, please see Carolyn Dunn's definitions in "Playing Indian" in this anthology.
4. See Jack Forbes, Columbus and Other Cannibals (New York: Autonomedia Publishers, 1992).

—

Acknowledgments

Bringing together a group of writers from different disciplines is never an easy task. This anthology includes the writings of social scientists, literary critics, activists, historians, and scholars from the humanities. I am indebted to the contributors to this volume for their patience, support, and invaluable insights into the study of cultural representation in contemporary Native communities. I would especially like to thank two of the contributors, Troy Johnson and Sara Sutler-Cohen, for reading through drafts of the entire manuscript and offering important feedback about content, structure, and organization.

Tomás Almaguer was also kind enough to read through and review the project and constantly gave me important feedback about the possible contributions this work could have in Native studies and ethnic studies. The generous financial support of the Ford Foundation postdoctoral fellowship program, the Vice President's Office at San Francisco State University, the Dean's Office in the College of Ethnic Studies at San Francisco State University, and the Sociology Department at the University of California, Santa Cruz, all provided me with the time, resources, and access to complete this project. I want to acknowledge my colleagues in the Departments of American Indian Studies and Ethnic Studies at San Francisco State for listening to my ideas and raising important questions about the significance of representation and contestation in Native communities. Many thanks to Howard Pinderhughes, Norma Alarcón, John Brown Childs, and Craig Reinarman for letters that helped me gain financial support that led to the development and completion of this project.

I am extremely indebted to the wonderful staff at AltaMira Press, especially to Senior Editor Rosalie Robertson for her suggestions, organization, and tremendous encouragement throughout this process.

Finally, I would like to thank my family. To my parents, Annetta and Kenneth Jolivétte, for always supporting me and believing in the purpose of my work and the value of higher education. To my siblings, Eric, Derick, Kevin, Makeba, Mary Rose, Nathan, and Charles, for mentoring and teaching me so much. And to Johnasies McGraw, for your love and patience and for reading through the many manuscript drafts . . . in you I have found everything.

Introduction

Andrew Jolivétte

The 2004 Grammy Award show was a not-so-subtle reminder of the implicit and explicit ways in which racial representations of Native Americans continue to be owned by non-Indians. When renowned hip-hop group OutKast took to the stage the crowd went wild. There was "whooping" and "hollering" from the stage, and tremendous applause from the crowd. The group's performance sparked controversy in the Native American community because Andre 3000 of OutKast and his entourage—like so many John Wayne movies—mimicked what many believe to be "traditional" Indian dress and dance. They donned ripped green clothing and leggings, the women wore next to nothing, and many of the performers sported feathers in their hair. The group has been hailed as one of the few in the hip-hop industry that have a positive and critical political angle, but for many fans this was a big letdown. The following fan's quote is taken from the online website *React Magazine*, which features news stories on hip-hop, R&B, and urban culture:

> Andre, Honestly what do you think you're doing? You used to be one of my favorite artists back in the day, and I'm not gonna hate on you simply because you're doing music I don't like, I have a much deeper reason for writing this letter. Your grammy performance this past Sunday has to be one of the single most offensive things shown on television in the past decade. CBS has said nothing, television critics have said nothing, but this cultural critic is going to say it, you let yourself become a minstrel. (posted February 10, 2004)

1

This response was just one perspective on the issue. In my sociology of race and ethnicity course many of my students were divided on the issue. Some fans knew nothing of the performance, while others were quickly dismayed by the reasons behind the controversy. Some students responded with disappointment while others said OutKast, like other professionals in the entertainment business, simply fell victim to the rules of the game, the status quo. For Native people this marked an important historical moment as many negative images about Indians have gone unchallenged, but in a defiant act of resistance and contestation over indigenous identity and representation Indian leaders said enough is enough. Andrew Brother Elk, chairman of the Native American Cultural Center in San Francisco, filed a complaint with the FCC; and the center, along with members of the Native community (as well as non-Native allies), began boycotting CBS because the media giant allowed the group to "commercialize Indian symbols," many of which are of a religious or spiritual nature (*React Magazine*).

OutKast performed in front of a fake tepee and wore headdresses and war paint, but many non-Indians might not understand the offense according to Brother Elk. "If people were wearing yarmulkes and the Hasidic dress and bumping and grinding, we would see that as ridiculous, but for some reason we don't see what OutKast did as ridiculous," Brother Elk said (*React Magazine*, 2004). Today this is just one of many cultural representations of American Indian people that gets used without a second thought as to how it might negatively shape the identities of indigenous people. The issue of Indian mascots, for example, has only been recently placed in an alternative historical context from Native peoples' perspective.

According to Ward Churchill, "bounties have been placed on the scalps of Indians—any Indians—in places as diverse as Georgia, Kentucky, Texas, the Dakotas, Oregon, and California, and had been maintained until resident Indian populations were decimated or disappeared altogether" (325). Churchill's comments are in reference to national football and baseball league officials and players who suggest that the use of Indian symbols and mascots is not harmful but is merely a way to "honor" Native Americans. Churchill goes on to explain:

A salient reason for public acquiescence before the ongoing holocaust in Native North America has been a continuation of the popular legacy, often through more effective media. Since 1925, Hollywood has released more than 2,000 films, many of them rerun on television, portraying Indians as strange, perverted, ridiculous, and often dangerous things of the past. Moreover, we are habitually presented to mass audiences one-dimensionally, devoid of recognizable human motivations and emotions; Indians thus serve as props, little more. We have thus been thoroughly and systematically dehumanized. (Churchill 327–328)

Static representations of Native Americans suggesting extinction or ethnic erasure are based on a complex combination of historic evidence on the one hand, and on inaccurate media and popular cultural representations in film, literature, and television on the other. For example, population estimates indicate that disease, war, and acts of violence against indigenous populations did lead to a population reduction of about 12 to 15 million in 1500 to 248,253 by 1890 (Nagel 5). Nagel goes on to argue that the media coverage of American Indian activism in the 1960s and 1970s led to an increased identification of the American population with their "Indian heritages":

We can also see a rather stable, though unsteadily growing Native American population during the first half of the twentieth century. What the table also shows, however, is a remarkable recovery of the American Indian population during the second half of the century. The number of Native Americans increased eightfold from 1900 to 1990, with much of the growth occurring in the decades after 1960, from the low point in 1900 to 523,591 in 1960 and to 1.88 million in 1990. (Nagel 5)

In 2000 the American Indian/Alaskan Native combined population reached 2,475,956 (U.S. Census 2000), indicating a steady increase, but why has there been such a tremendous increase unexplained by demographic data? Some scholars such as Nagel suggest it's economics and increased public visibility due to American Indian activism from 1960 to 1980. Despite this renewed population growth and visibility, Natives still only constitute 0.9 percent of total U.S. population (U.S. Census 2000), an important reminder that demographic numbers often can ensure disenfranchisement.

Today, contrary to emerging themes, "all Indians" aren't rich from gambling casinos or golf resorts. Most Indians do pay taxes, and perhaps most important, Indian tribes are unique, autonomous political entities, nation-states, not ethnic minorities in the same way as other groups such as Latinos, African Americans, and Asian Americans. Yes, indigenous people experience racism, subordinate group status, and economic oppression as do other ethnic minorities, but many tribes with state and federal recognition (and many of those without recognition) have established treaties that protect their rights to self-determination and self-governance. Unfortunately most Americans do not know that tribal sovereignty preceded the development of the U.S. Constitution. In fact, according to the American Indian Policy Center:

> The framers of the United States Constitution specifically recognized the sovereignty of Indian tribes. In Article 1, Section 8, clause 3 of the Constitution, Congress is identified as the governmental branch authorized to regulate commerce with "foreign nations, among several states, *and with the Indian tribes* [italics added]." The Supreme Court reaffirmed this legal and political standing of Indian nations in a set of three 19th Century court decisions known as the Marshall Trilogy. These cases serve as cornerstones to understanding Indian sovereignty in the U.S. political system as a clearly defined legal status that has constitutional standing. (Pevar 1992)

There have been different interpretations however, about the clarity and stability of basing tribal sovereignty on the U.S. government's Constitution and laws. Some argue that it is this same dependence on U.S. policy that has allowed hundreds of tribes to continue to go unrecognized by the U.S. government and that this also leads to underfunding for these tribes. The problem of recognition is notably pronounced in California where tribes have smaller populations, are located in urban areas, or do not fit into the U.S. government's definition of what counts as Indian. On the other hand, there are those who argue that the only way to protect the rights of tribes (including the unrecognized tribes in California and in other states) is by forcing the U.S. government to abide by its own laws with regard to tribes that have established treaties. This is a difficult task because of Congress's refusal to comply with treaties that were signed between the United States and hundreds of Indian Nations. According to the *Sacramento Bee* the problem has not only led to underrepresentation and invisibility but has also forced many of these tribes into poverty:

> If Indians seem invisible, it's because their identity has been buried by an avalanche of federal policies designed to absorb Indians into mainstream society. Ever since California became American soil in 1848, the United States has shortchanged California's Indians more than any other American Indians. A six-month investigation by The Bee found that today, the average California Indian owns less land, has less money, gets less federal aid, has access to less health care and education, is less likely to have a job and gets less justice than other Indians nationwide. Because most of California's Indians have been stripped of their land or funneled into California's cities from other states, they don't officially exist and are cut off from millions in federal aid that other American Indians routinely receive. In 1992, Congress conceded that "government policies and programs affecting California Indians" have resulted in "a continuing social and economic crisis, characterized by . . . alcoholism and substance abuse, critical health problems, family violence and child abuse, lack of educational and employment opportunities, and significant barriers to tribal economic development." (American Indian Policy Center website)

It is important to remember that under the Marshall Trilogy,[1] trust responsibility is integral to the concept of tribal sovereignty. The trust responsibility is based on negotiations between tribes that bound the United States and requires the United States to represent the best interest of tribes, to protect the safety and well-being of tribal members, and to fulfill its treaty obligations, responsibilities, and commitments (American Indian Policy Center). The idea behind this agreement is that Indians trust the United States to follow through on promises that were made through treaties in exchange for land (Pevar 1992: 26).

Despite this unique status, many Native People are still the victims of violence, still live in poverty at alarming rates—much higher than the national average—and experience cultural theft of art and religion. Perhaps most damaging, the images and cultural representations that have so much impact on how Native People are viewed today are based on misinformation that indigenous peoples have little or no control over in any significant way. It is with this in mind that the "Indian Nations Strike Back" (to borrow from *Star Wars* and Edward Said) by articulating new frameworks for understanding the impact of social, legal, economic, literary, and cultural representations on Indian people's well-being.

This collection of essays then, is a critical response to contemporary issues facing Native populations in North America. The title for the this project, *Cultural Representation in Native America*, is about a critical cultural shift and movement away from boundaries and fixed representational categories within Native studies and within larger societal contexts. The issues range from media images and mascots, to indigenous literature, Native American Barbie dolls, and mixed-race identity in the new millennium from the U.S.-Mexican border, Las Vegas, and North Dakota to the bayous of Louisiana. *Cultural Representation in Native America* speaks to the work being done by academics and activists to renarrate and rearticulate the images of Indian people's history, religion, identity, and oral and literary traditions, and the current state of social, political, and cultural representation within and outside of Native communities. The project therefore provides a space for rethinking regional boundaries and limitations on where and how indigenous communities are remembered, revitalized, constructed, and preserved.

The contributors to this collection contest the static and essentialized discourse on Native American people through insightful research, personal experiences, and an intensive dialectical process that will engage other Native and non-Native people. More importantly the ideas, expressions, poetry, lived experiences, and social histories contained within these pages speak directly to undergraduate and graduate students who can make a difference in the cultural production of images that exploit American Indians in U.S. society.

Part I, Contestation and Representation, deals with contemporary examples of popular cultural depictions of Native People. The discussion begins in chapter 1, "Mapping Contests in Unknown Locations," an essay by Paula Gunn Allen that weaves personal narrative and oral tradition with insightful historical recollections to demonstrate the growth in interest about "all things Indian" since the 1960s and 1970s. From powwows to the current craze over Indian jewelry, art, and literature, Gunn Allen takes the reader on a journey through history that reads like an intricate poem, almost rhythmically capturing the essence of how the U.S. public sphere has been dramatically reshaped by the ability of non-Indians to "go Native." Chapter 2, "Say Hau to Native American Barbie" by Kim Shuck, is a provocative piece about the expansion of the Mattel collection of ethnic Barbie dolls, with a specific analysis of how the dolls attempt to portray American Indian culture and the importance of these dolls as cultural signifiers to children both Native and non-Native alike. Chapter 3, "Liquor Moccasins" by Philip Klasky, takes a brief and personal look at the use of American Indian dolls in Las Vegas and juxtaposes these visual images with the silence surrounding acts of nuclear and environmental warfare on indigenous people in the same geographic region. Chapter 4, "(Dis)Locating Spiritual Knowledge," builds upon the previous chapter themes of Indian cultural representation, authenticity, and commodification as it relates to spirituality and the emergence of non-Native (and some Native) impostors who are marketing themselves as authentic "healers" and "shamans." Sara Sutler-Cohen's research is meticulous and offers a fresh perspective on a sensitive and often overlooked subject. The fifth and final essay in this section, "Masks in the New Millennium" by Winona LaDuke, examines the controversy at University of North Dakota over the use of the mascot name "the Fighting Sioux." LaDuke carefully narrates the unfolding political debates at North Dakota, but more importantly she offers new insight into the political, religious, and economic factors that play into the preservation of Indian mascots.

Part II, Contestation and Politics, focuses more specifically on policy and the legal issues related to American Indian sovereign status and protection under the U.S. Constitution. Troy Johnson's explication of the roots of American Indian revitalization and activism in the post–World War II era is an important account of the roles that women and men played in reshaping U.S. legislation related to Indian affairs as well as the effects of relocation to urban areas. In chapter 6, "Native American Resistance and Revitalization in the Era of Self-Determination," Johnson astutely connects the activist resistance of the 1960s and 1970s with current U.S. policy as it relates to Indian self-determination. In chapter 7, "Oral Tradition, Identity, and Intergenerational Healing through the Southern Paiute Salt Songs," Melissa Nelson examines religious, political, and oral traditions to intricately and critically dispel the myth that Native people and their traditions are vanishing. In this case the Southern Paiute are Nelson's case study. Chapter 8, "In the Spirit of Crazy Horse," addresses the political stakes involved in the use of the name and image of famous Sioux Chief Tasunke Witko (also known as Crazy Horse). Winona LaDuke offers an important historical context as she effectively outlines the legal strategies used by the descendants of Crazy Horse to prevent beer companies from continuing to use the name and image of Crazy Horse as a form of commercialization and profit.

Part III, Contestation and Mixed-Race Identity, deals with perhaps one of the most pressing contemporary socioeconomic issues facing Native Americans today: racial identity and the impact of miscegenation on individual and legal identification as Indian. Chapter 9, "In the Tracks of 'the' Native Woman," explores the exploitation of indigenous women of Spanish and Indian descent on both sides of the U.S.-Mexican border. Norma Alarcón asserts that the Chicana woman's journey for an identity that will empower rather than mask her ability to possess her own subjectivity is based on nationalistic and patriarchal discourse that renders the Native, the Indian woman silent. Alarcón suggests that contemporary Chicanas are embracing and rearticulating a mestiza consciousness that is inclusive of their indigenous ancestry. Chapter 10, "Chapped with Weather and Age: Mixed-Blood Identity and the Shape of History," is the personal family story of Sara Sutler-Cohen, who discusses her journey of dealing with the conflicts and joys of being a mixed blood and the internal dialectical processes at work for mixed-blood Indians and the descendants of Indians that are often different for so many other racially mixed people in the United States.

Carolyn Dunn's "Playing Indian" focuses on the Native American literary tradition and its treatment of mixed-blood themes. Her discussion of the oral tradition and of contemporary Native American literature as one of the community's most popular art forms and sites of resistance/representation sharply contrasts indigenous American Indian and African trickster themes, mixed-blood identity, and the often invisible nature of Native American literature from the discipline of English literature despite the growth and popularization of Native writers over the last thirty years. In the final essay, "Examining the Regional and Multigenerational Context of Creole and American Indian Identity," I argue that the face of

Native American communities is changing, and with that shift the representations must also change, whether physical/biological/ phenotypical, literary, philosophical, or media related. I use Creoles of Color from the state of Louisiana as a case study to explore the issues and themes related to including and excluding mixed-blood communities in the indigenous community's struggle for self-identification/determination.

If the majority of the Indian population will be/is already racially mixed, then we must question which "types of mixtures" are getting included/excluded. We must also explore why a (re)mapping of how we locate and articulate indigenous identity as diasporic[2] can sustain our communities for future generations.

Together, this collection draws upon the most salient contemporary issues of representation and contestation that continue to prevent Native People from deciding how they get defined, if they get defined, and how to interpret these complex definitions. This project is one of the first to look specifically at the issue of American Indian representation in the twentieth and twenty-first centuries from an interdisciplinary framework. It offers a new and critical interpretation of social and legal policy, an examination of popular culture, and a provocative analysis of identity through multiple lenses. What is offered here is the collective contribution of a new voice and perspective on contemporary Native American studies.

Notes

1. The Marshall Trilogy is the name for the three U.S. Supreme Court cases that reaffirmed the legal and political rights of Indian nations. These three cases: *Johnson v. McIntosh* (1823), *Cherokee Nation v. Georgia* (1831), and *Worcester v. Georgia* (1832) respectively held that tribal sovereignty, though impaired by European colonization, cannot be dismissed because Indians are the original inhabitants of the United States; Indians were a distinct political society, separated from others, capable of managing their own affairs and governing themselves; and finally tribal sovereign authority is not relinquished when Indian tribes exchange land for peace or protection (Getches et al. 1979).

2. By diasporic I refer to a concept used in my dissertation where I argue that indigenous peoples are diasporic because of their forced removal from tribal lands, which was involuntary. I also assert that some of the

movement of indigenous peoples (especially among mixed-race populations like the Creole population) was voluntary, but also was done as
a means of self-preservation. The concept also refers to the ways that
indigenous peoples' movement to urban areas (through the relocation
program) has led to the re-creation of the communities in different regions nationally and internationally, primarily through ethnic enclaves,
social clubs, and other organizations.

References

American Indian Policy Center website: www.airpi.org/index.html,
   accessed June 2004.
Churchill, Ward. "Crimes Against Humanity," in *Race, Class, and Gender*,
   edited by Margaret Andersen and Patricia Hill Collins. Belmont, CA:
   Wadsworth Publishing, 2004.
Getches, David H., Daniel M. Rosenfelt, and Charles F. Wilkinson.
   Federal Indian Law: Cases and Materials. St. Paul: West, 1979.
Nagel, Joane. *American Indian Ethnic Renewal*. Oxford: Oxford University
   Press, 1997.
Pevar, Stephen. *The Rights of Indians and Tribes: The Authoritative ACLU
   Guide to Indian Tribal Rights*. Carbondale: Southern Illinois University
   Press, 1992.
React Magazine, posted online message, February 10, 2004. www
   .ReactMag.com.
U.S. Census Bureau website: www.census.gov/main/www/census2000
   .html, accessed June 2004.

I

CONTESTATION
AND REPRESENTATION

1

Mapping Contests in Unknown Locations

Paula Gunn Allen

[The Invisible Race
[Nos Venceremos
[And Then There Were None
[The Shakespearean Construction of American Indian History
Here We Go Again
Dateline: Sacramento, California. October 7, 2003

ARNOLD Schwarzenegger was elected Governor of California after a bitter media-staged battle to recall the former Governor, the uncharismatic Gray Davis. Schwarzenegger ran on a platform characterized as the latest in a war that has raged for five centuries. The self-styled *Terminator* from Austria caught the crest of the tsunami wave of anger that had been swelling for two years and had no real target. While it is a nation-wide disaster, California was one of the few places people had a target to rage at. Shrewdly, Schwarzenegger, himself an immigrant, knew how to ride that wave. He did what others coming to these shores had done for centuries: targeted Indians and Mexicans. The surefire strategy was bound to sweep him into office. Particularly as it was mostly waged on screen, where the most popular battles between Indians and Northern Europeans have taken place. It worked so well for John Wayne and Ronald Reagan it couldn't fail to work for him!

Inside sources have informed this reporter that the next step in the latest stage of the centuries long war is to declare Indian

13

casinos ungodly. Other reliable sources report that the Governor will declare Indian casinos a health hazard and will require that they be shut down. . . .

The Invisibility Function

The other night upon the stair
I saw a man who wasn't there.
He wasn't there again today.
I wish that man would go away.

When I was growing up we were pretty visible, albeit exotic. The verges of Highway 66 were dotted with small stands made of pine branches and roofed with boughs. They served to protect the women who sat beneath them from the sun as they spent the day roadside offering the pots they had made during the winter months. In the late 1940s and early 1950s, traffic was often dense along the long two-lane highway—the famed link between St. Louis, Missouri, and L.A. Maybe you remember the song about it; maybe you and your folks drove it, reading Burma Shave signs and roasting in cars that didn't have air conditioning. They had only recently been able to buy sufficient gasoline to keep them going the hundreds of miles many of them traveled.

It was in the 1950s that President Dwight D. Eisenhower decreed that the interstates be built in order to facilitate flight from urban centers in the event of nuclear war. Another Eisenhower decree was something that Congress would authorize as HCR 108, known as the Termination Act. In an eerie foreshadowing of events in California, the president announced, "It's time to get out of the Indian business." Fifty years later the would-be governor of California demanded that Indians get out of the Indian business as well. "It's time they paid taxes like the rest of us," he shouted.

As the 1950s turned into the 1960s, Indian people in New Mexico disappeared. Of course we were still quite present . . . in the Pueblo villages, on the Navajo and Apache reservations, even in urban enclaves in the larger towns. But unless you knew where Indian Country, New Mexico, was, you'd never know it was there.

There were exceptions, of course. While the United States was going about the business of divesting itself of its legally sworn obligations to domestic-sovereign nations, Anglo business people in a large variety of venues were making a buck. The postcard industry flourished, and there was brisk trade in newly made Indian jewelry and its more lucrative sibling, Indian pawn. Navajo rugs, Apache baskets, Pueblo pottery, even toy tomahawks, children's rubber-topped "Indian" drums, an occasional buckskin-clad doll, often as not sold nearly alongside the far more valuable kachina dolls. These wares graced gas station windows, trading company shelves, curio shops, and cafés and diners along 66 from Santa Rosa, New Mexico, in the east to Kingman, Arizona, in the west and from Raton, New Mexico, in the north to El Paso, Texas, in the south.

These signs of tom-toms and tepees, themselves all too evident in billboards and neon lights, no doubt fueled the local economies more than any other industry, including cattle or wool growing. However, one could at least see that Indian country hadn't disappeared at the "First Thanksgiving," though the visibility was confined to the Southwest. For while there were Native communities in almost every corner of the United States, Indians had vanished from the American scene and consciousness. Even the fact that at least a third of the names of places, including street names, in the country—particularly on the Atlantic seaboard—were Native names or words seems to have escaped notice. And while American arts and letters along with its entertainment industry were rife with Indians, they were collected safely in the past. Indians became America's heritage, not a diverse population of several hundred communities spread from north to south, from coast to coast. You'd think we had all died.

By 1976 when the country celebrated its bicentennial, Indians had gone to the happy hunting grounds soon after sharing a turkey dinner with English people somewhere on the northeastern seaboard. At any rate that was how it seemed to those of us watching the celebrations on television and reading short versions of the short history of the United States put out by various bicentennial groups. Nor was the situation in American history or literature classes any better. When I was in attendance at the University of New Mexico in the early 1960s, I don't remember a mention of Indians in the survey of United States literature I took, unless it was the astonishingly hateful bit penned by Samuel Clemens (Mark Twain).

The mojo Ike put on his declaration of the end of Indian business must have been pretty heavy: In a very few years everybody disappeared, and not until the rise of Indian gaming has our presence been publicly recognized—and this time it's us doing the promoting. Perhaps that's why Schwarzenegger and his moolah-stuffed backers found it convenient to attack. It worked for Ike, why not for Aah-nold? Oh, dear. I can barely imagine what it's going to cost the heavily indebted state of California to realize Schwarzenegger's demand. The Native People don't have to take it anymore, at least not to the extent that was horrifyingly required in the 1950s. In fact, it might have been the Termination Act that added the greatest impetus to the present remembering of life in Indian Country then, and may well be the new wave assault that will act as catalyst for Indians to take back our identities.

In the early 1970s I was driving with my brother to the coast along the new I-40 that had mostly replaced Highway 66. Stopping in Gallup for lunch, we pulled into the small Sheraton Inn. Walking into the lobby we nodded at the desk clerks, a longhaired blond young woman and a blond young man. Proceeding to the coffee shop we were soon seated. Our order was taken by an Hispanic young woman, and the other waiter on duty was also Hispanic. Lee says, "I bet the dishwasher is Indian. Watch this." He beckoned the server over and asked her something about where she had gotten the necklace or earrings she had on. They were made of juniper seeds spaced between coral beads. She said that the dishwasher's mother made them. He was Navajo.

In the mid-1980s I went to Coronado Mall in Albuquerque. I had been living on the coast for some time, and this was a winter visit home. To my surprise—and delight—I saw a satisfying variety of Indians among the shoppers: Pueblos, Navajos, "urban Indians"— the lot. I knew who was which by dress. Often a group of Pueblo shoppers would have among them at least one dressed in traditional style. Mainly, the hairstyle of both women and men identified them. Other Pueblos and many Navajo shoppers wore Levis, Stetsons, working cowboy boots (they have a low heel). Urban Indians were dressed in down jackets, often as not brown ones, and either knitted caps or baseball caps. Shops, cafés, the covered walkways—we were, like Simon Ortiz had commented the decade before, everywhere. People who were obviously Indian were eating in restaurants, sitting around in posh cocktail lounges, driving up the streets and down the avenues in Japanese-made cars, as well as, of course, the traditional Chevy pickups, locally known as "Indian Cadillacs."

Similarly, in the mid-1970s I took my mother to our Feast Day at Santa Ana Pueblo for the first time. We went because the Santa Ana Feast Day was also her birthday. That time there were maybe a dozen or so men and women dancing. (Despite their small numbers, they danced the rain into the pueblo—this on a hot day in late July when rain had been scarce and no fronts were predicted by meteorologists.) A few years later we went again and we could hardly get into the village the traffic was so heavy, and having gotten there found the Plaza crowded with at least a hundred dancers and crowds of onlookers.

What had happened? From a traditional point of view, I can say the gods came back, for that or something very like it had happened. Clearly the cosmic clock had moved into a time of renewal for Native Peoples, and this was not only in New Mexico but across the United States, Canada, and many if not most countries south of the U.S. border. Of course, there are many other, more Anglo-rational explanations, not the least among them being the temper of the times in the United States and elsewhere.

Certainly a case can be made for the impact of the civil rights movement on the new visibility of Native People, books, magazines, and journals; for the rising fame of Indian artists; for the cognoscenti's renewed interest in exotica at home, backed up by the stupendous rise in income of the privileged classes. A case can also be made for the impact of Indian lawyers and non-Indian lawyers specializing in Indian law, a special branch of American jurisprudence. It is a branch, by the way, that few Americans know about. Based in treaty law, stemming from legal agreements the U.S. government has made with the Native nations over the past century or so, it defines the legal status of Native nations as sovereign. It is this body of law, and the formidable array of attorneys experienced in trying cases brought against Native nations by any other governmental agency, individual, group, or business.

It is that body of law that the California state government will have to take on should the reckless new governor attempt to make good on his campaign threat. The chances that the state of California would lose should they go to court to compel California tribal nations to pay taxes on casino income are enormous. The costs to the heavily indebted state would force it into bankruptcy given its present state of fiscal devastation because the case could drag on for years. Admittedly, power-grabbing Americans find it difficult, if not impossible, to cope with the idea—never mind the fact—that we ain't the BIA's Indians anymore.

Americans, when they think of us at all, prefer us to be objects of pity, and that means impoverished beyond even the lower limits of impoverishment among the rest of Americans from lower income groups. Admittedly it's pleasant indeed (or so I hear) to bask in one's virtue when sending used clothing to the poor Indians at the mission. And, admittedly, many find it annoying in the extreme—downright reality-shattering—to consider that Native Peoples might be able to fight back, in the courts, in terms of bank accounts, in terms of growing self-respect and economic/political clout, and win. And retain sovereignty and identity as First Nations people in the bargain! "Oh, bother," said Pooh.

This fall I went to a powwow in Austin, Texas with a friend I was visiting. I wanted to be there in time for the Grand Entry and would have been, but the booths outside the gym where the dancing was going on were a big distraction. I have felt, ever since my first powwow experience, that every opportunity to powwow should be taken because only there can a Californian get fry bread and do some shopping not available at the mall. Of course, the music is great, too.

At the booths I was captivated by the new stuff for sale, by new items in older categories of stuff, and by the large number of booths. We browsed for quite a while, then knew we were missing the best part of the evening. Asking one of the Indian stall keepers where to get the best fry bread, we headed for the gym, arriving in time to miss the Gourd Dancing, another favorite, as well as the Grand Entry. Nevertheless, we were in the stands in time to stand for the honoring song for those serving in Iraq. The honor guard was composed of veterans from a number of American conflicts from World War II, Korea, Vietnam, the Persian Gulf, and other military postings. The company was Cherokee, and they carried the Cherokee Nation flag along with the flag of the United States and the flag of Texas.

It's a strange experience to be moved to tears and pride, to honor those so far from home and all those who died for a country they see as their own lands to defend, while simultaneously being antiwar and in any mainstream setting entirely unmoved by such displays. I was particularly aware of the ambiguity of my situation (a fairly normal occurrence, really) because I was accompanied by my friend who is not Native, and who is very liberal in all things. I had received a chain e-mail early in this latest American foray into armed conflict from someone in South Dakota whose brother had been sent over. The letter asked that recipients pray for the young man and send the letter along to others. Foolishly, I sent it to one person I thought was simpatico. It had been illustrated with a beautiful icon of a flying eagle, and the artwork alone was impressive to me. At any rate my correspondent returned it immediately with a sharp rebuff. It seems that she was antiwar, and I guess that meant anti-soldiers-staying-alive. Odd.

The first time I went to a powwow was in the mid-1970s in California. My uncle offered to take me to a powwow that was being held in San Jose, maybe at the fair grounds there. I had never been to a powwow, though of course I had attended dances at the pueblos, particularly at Laguna. I suppose I imagined something similar would be happening at the powwow. My uncle was all dressed out in his ice cream pants and velvet Navajo-style shirt, his hair tied back in a bun at the nape of his neck, his head bound with a large handkerchief folded in the Pueblo-Navajo men's way. He was wearing moccasins and had brought a blanket to wear folded over one arm. I was wearing my usual garb—jeans, moccasins, a light shirt—and carrying the Pueblo-style shawl I always wore in those days. My uncle noticed the shawl and remarked that it was a good thing I'd brought it so I could dance, too. That was the first bit of powwow etiquette I was to learn.

At this powwow I was completely disoriented. I had no idea that people would be dancing around in a large circle rather than in lines like we do at home, or that there would be men sitting around a huge drum, each moving his stick simultaneously to bring it down at the same time. I certainly wasn't prepared for what the men were wearing, or for what the women were wearing, for that matter. I can say that no one was dressed the way I thought they should/would be. You see, at home the dancers form lines, and the drums are small hand drums carried by men who take up the rear of the lines of dancers. The men are dressed in kilts, sometimes bare-chested, other times with shirts, and the kilts are similar to loin cloths but are woven of thick woolen thread and embroidered with a particular pattern in red and green or red and white. They always wear the kind of bells on their ankles that reindeer who accompany Santa wear, and the sound of the steps is—I don't know—familiar, transporting? It's the rain, of course.

The women wear mantas, knee-length black tunic-cut dresses that are joined at one shoulder. The other shoulder is bare, or would have been in times past. Since old man missionary came out our way, the mantas serve as an overdress to a straight cotton dress with a high Peter Pan collar and sport small ruffles at cuff and hem. The sleeves and hem are ornamented with bright rickrack or decorative ribbon, and it opens slightly at the neck to allow it to be pulled on over one's head. The manta is cinched with a beautiful woven woolen belt, about three inches wide. It too is woven in a pattern with red and green thread and small areas of white. The mantas are also made of wool, usually of a fine grade so they are lightweight.

Over this attire is worn a cape called an utinatz, a large ladies head scarf lined with broad satin ribbon that extends several inches at the ends so it can be tied around the neck loosely. The sides of the black overdress, the manta, are held together with silver buttons, traditionally made of silver money—dimes if you're poor, silver dollars if you are very well-to-do. I think now these fasteners are silver and turquoise, as well as more traditional coins. The final piece a woman wears is a fine half-apron, tied around her waist. These are ornate; they are dress-up aprons, not cooking-in aprons.

The one I had was white cotton with a wide band of cotton lace tatting running between the top and bottom halves. My under dress was two dresses, one white and the other red, with open-cut diamonds on the white overdress (worn under the manta, of course) that allowed the red beneath to show. In the old times the women and men wore Laguna moccasins, a particular cut of shoe with hard soles that curl up in a point at the toe and reach up over the ankles. Made of deer hide, they are light gray and have a wide flap that is fastened with a silver concho on the side. When I was young most of the dancers wore tennis shoes. The women often wore those heavy cotton stockings that rural women wore until well after World War II. The men usually wore their kilts over their levis, and always wore shirts.

Of course, there are dances other than the "corn dance" at the Pueblos. Two of the more spectacular are the Hoop Dance and the Eagle Dance, though Deer Dance is astonishing and so is Buffalo Dance. The young women's Butterfly Maidens is a lovely dance, and the girls I've seen doing it always look so earnest and proud of their fine regalia. That was the sort of scene I had pictured in my mind as we entered the dance grounds outside San Jose and parked. I was soon disabused of my provincial ideas.

The distance between what I expected and what I encountered was as great as that between Pueblo and Plains Indians' worlds. What was even odder was that our encounter was taking place far from both homelands: We weren't in South Dakota or New Mexico. We were in San Jose, California, a few miles south of the San Francisco Bay Area. There was not a California Indian in sight; I mean everyone was dressed Plains, though powwow is an Algonquin word that means "we dream together." There was one drum and maybe thirty or forty dancers. Although their regalia was strange to my Pueblo eyes, it certainly was colorful. The men wore small, narrow headdresses that looked like brushy hair standing straight up from the center of their heads. This shock of hair was connected to a beaded edging that I thought was tied around it to hold it up like a brushy ponytail. Eventually I noticed that it was fastened to ties that were secured under the chin and realized that the "hair" wasn't the head hair of the dancers. I asked my uncle about it, and he told me it's called a roach. Seeing my look of doubt and confusion, he laughed. We were in the Bay Area, after all. "Not that kind of roach," he grinned.

Like the Pueblo men, these wore kilts—though they were adorned with beaded Plains or Woodlands designs rather than with cross-stitch Pueblo patterns—and long-sleeved shirts, upper arms banded with leather beaded bands about four inches wide. The most eye-catching items, though, were the feathered shields they wore fastened at mid-back and buttocks. These items, known as bustles, looked like sunwheels. The centers, about eight inches in diameter, were beaded and from them radiated a perfect circle of feathers, dyed Day-Glo pink or yellow. Most of the men also wore moccasins, and their ankles were circled by the jingle bells also worn at Pueblo dances. So even though the scene was alien to my eyes, the sound was comforting and familiar.

The women danced demurely, circling the drum, the men fancy dancing, as it's called, around the perimeter. All the women wore shawls over their dresses or jeans and shirts, and footwear was varied, mostly sports shoes. The woman's step is a very subdued hop that looks almost like a walk. Indeed, many of the women walk. But male and female, the dancers move to the drum and the song and, at intervals that are not regular in metric time, stop, then make a certain cross-step when the movement continues, calm, dignified, entirely present.

To my eye, the roles played by each, male and female, are exactly right: for the male is quick and transitory, exciting and powerful like the jagged lightning that flashes earthward during an electric storm. The female is not only subdued but oblivious to the male tumult around her. The men dance in isolation, each some distance from all the rest, male and female. But the women dance in loosely structured clusters, not quite rows, that morph as the circling goes on. Often they are dancing near friends and relatives, exchanging low comments in the kind of stately promenade that, in my mind, is the perfectly self-contained circling of the planets about the sun. The contrast, knitted together by the drum and every dancer's attentive focus on the song, is deeply satisfying. It's home, if home is the place of the comfortableness of a complete heart.

That was my first powwow. My latest, the one in Austin in late October 2003, could hardly have been more different. Not because the outfits and kinds of dancing differed but because the regalia had rediscovered itself. By then I had attended many powwows and had long since felt as at home with the northern and southern Plains drums as with Corn Dance. The regalia was no longer strange, either, but it had changed profoundly in the thirty years since San Jose. Another major change was in the girls' and women's fancy dancing. Fancy dancing has always been something men do. It is a series of steps where right foot crosses behind or before left, and the steps are reversed. Exactly when the change is made seems to depend on the dancer himself, but as I have never done it, I don't exactly know. The men's body motions resemble birds on the ground, courting—it is mesmerizing when done well.

There were five drums, some southern, some northern. There was an honoring dance for war veterans so powerful tears sprang to my eyes. There were dancers, outfitted in dazzling array. There were fancy dancers, male and female. Some of the former were very young, while others were definitely elders. The female fancy dancers were all young, and some of them excelled at this relatively new art. I remember when the young women began to fancy dance. My niece, then in her late teens, was among several young women who were determined to fancy dance. It was the 1970s, and women's lib was sweeping the land. These young women convinced the dance teacher at the Indian Center in San Francisco to teach them. I don't remember how long it was from that time until the girls and young women began to appear at powwow, dancing along the fringes of the throng, doing the cross-stepping that is the sign of that kind of dance. They didn't wear bustles and roaches, of course. They wore jingle dresses, buckskin, cloth dresses Plains or Woodlands style. They each carried a beaded feather fan in one hand, a beaded bag in the other, with a shawl folded into a rectangle and draped over one arm, beaded moccasins, and a beaded headband. Most had long hair worn in braids.

The men's regalia had changed perhaps more profoundly: the feathers, headdresses, fans, moccasins, armbands, kilts were breathtaking. Brown, black and white, grey—the colors of the feathers on bustles and fans had become subdued, and many wore elaborate headdresses instead of roaches. Some were made of fur with foxtails hanging down. This was not the first huge powwow I had attended, of course. I had attended one in Albuquerque with my mother in the 1980s that stays fresh in my mind. It was held at the convention center. The dance floor was at the center of the space surrounded by rising rows of bleachers. We got there in time for the Grand Opening, and the dancers, led by head woman and head man, began to enter in their proper order, the flag bearers hoisting both the flag of the United States and the flag of the State of New Mexico, and behind them in pairs, moving sedately onto the floor, hundreds of women, men, young people, the lot. The leaders slowly circled the dance floor, moving in ever decreasing spirals until the first dancers were moving in a small, tight group at the center, and although the floor seemed full to me, dancers continued to enter. It was the most amazing Grand Entry I have ever seen. Memorable for the hundreds of dancers, it was also memorable to me because I worried how they would exit should there be some sudden need to evacuate the building. I'm not sure, but I think it was the first powwow my mother had attended, and she was properly impressed. I think she was as blown away as I was at the multitude; I'm sure I can't imagine her thoughts or feelings as we sat and watched them wheel below us for a few hours.

We also shopped, of course, beginning with the fry bread booth where we got "Navajo tacos," and then we made our way around the gallery of stands that lined the mezzanine level of the huge building. Vendors from around the country were there, Indian and white. One I remember was Shoshone, and we fell to talking about the role of women in traditional and modern Indian communities. He told me a couple of stories about women in leadership positions among his people who live in the Colorado Rockies, I think. *The Sacred Hoop*, my book about American Indian women, literature, and movements, had been published around then, and he, as well as a couple of other vendors I spoke with, had read it. It seems that it was a thumbs-up judgment from these men, something that relieved me greatly. Indeed, over the years I have seldom run into Indian men who question my point, which is basically that in a large number of Native communities, traditionally women held positions of power and were viewed with esteem and respect by their male counterparts.

The booths in Austin, as well as at other powwows I have attended, offer a great deal that speaks of thriving presence in postmodern America. One item I always seek out is bumper stickers and posters. Some of my favorites are clear indicators that we're still here, and not going anywhere else in the foreseeable future. My favorite at Austin was a poster that depicted four Indian men, very modern, very Rez, dark glasses, long hair, black Stetsons or handkerchief headbands, tee shirts, jeans, rifles. The caption read, "Homeland Security, 500 years." It put me in mind of the many pointed comments at powwows, on cars, and hanging in living rooms, dorm rooms, bedrooms across Indian country I've enjoyed over the years since the San Jose powwow. Some that I still enjoy, just remembering them, include "Custer Wore Arrow Shirts," "Indian Affairs Are the Best," and "If You're Indian You're IN."

But slogans aren't the only pop-culture signs of a renaissance of Indian presence throughout this land. Tapes and now CDs that offer a broad range of Indian music from all parts of the country, and all periods of Indian music, from traditional to hip-hop, are on offer at the powwow booths. Then there's the books, poetry, travel books, fiction, political books, histories, storytelling collections, comics, philosophy. . . . As an inveterate reader I am always delighted to see the offerings—new ones and old friends—available to powwow goers. Then there's the art. . . . Oh, man, is there art. I think that one of the most irritating things about not having oodles of cash comes crashing in on me when I see some of the art on display. I have never been to a decent-size powwow where I didn't see at least three or four paintings or art posters I coveted. Along with the jewelry, from silver and turquoise of the Southwest to beadwork of the Plains, the offerings grow in quantity and improve in workmanship. I was raised in New Mexico, and Indian arts—fine or those designated "crafts"—have always surrounded me. From a lifetime of living with and seeing Indian jewelry, I think I have developed an eye for it, and to my eye some of the jewelry sold at powwows is awesome, and that that isn't, trinkets, inexpensive bits and bobs, has increased quantums in range and style. What else? Well, there's the clothing . . . many T-shirts and sweatshirts that are themselves works of art; women's shawls, dresses, accessories; men's arm bands and roaches; men's and women's fans and moccasins . . . the kinds and qualities of things for sale has turned every good powwow into an Indian mall.

What all of this abundance signifies is that Indian Country is alive and well in America. There are many indicators of this, of course; from nationally known writers, artists, musicians, potters, weavers, and designers to casinos to growing visibility of Indian Americans in a variety of venues, the presence of Indians in twenty-first-century life is sufficiently marked to force recognition at a number of levels in modern global society. In the late 1990s, N. Scott Momaday was nominated for a Nobel Prize for Literature. While it went to an Italian man whose name I don't remember, the presence of American Indian literature as a major literary force was noted at global levels. In California, at least, one sees Indian paintings, or good lithographic copies of them, in all kinds of places. Doctors' and dentists' offices, banks, psychotherapists, hospitals, hotel corridors and lobbies . . . our work, like ourselves, is everywhere.

I don't mean to suggest that we don't have severe problems that must be met. I do mean to suggest, though, that we seem to be doing just that. Painfully, slowly, almost invisibly, and ever persistently, we remain, a presence in the Americas and in the world. Not bad for a people said to have passed along with the rest of the natural world, buried under a sea of chemicals and disease. The powwow and other dances are, to my mind, a major indicator of the strength of Indian persistence. I believe that persistence, and not resistance, is what kept us ourselves over these dreadful centuries. The people just kept on keepin' on, as one Indian bumper sticker I saw in the 1970s put it, and as the twentieth century drew to its close, the stubborn persistence was yielding huge benefits . . . not the least of which is lots of light, fluffy, pale golden brown fry bread.

2

Say Hau to Native American Barbie

Kim Shuck

For the last three years or so I have been using American Indian/ Native American Barbie dolls as teaching resources. I taught oral literature in the American Indian Studies Department at San Francisco State University, and my students were generally a pretty savvy group. I feel that it is important not only to go over a historical view of Indian oral tradition—creation cycles and the like—but also to view some of the stories that are told about Native people. By the time Barbie makes her debut in my class, we have talked a bit about stereotypes, gone over some light history of the United States, and discussed some of the ways in which an oral literature is passed along. When I pull my Barbie out of her paper sack, everyone in the class has expectations. Barbie occupies an iconic position in U.S. culture. My students expect that I will completely trash the dolls and their maker. I actually find them fascinating.

Make no mistake; there is no way in which Mattel has accurately or even respectfully represented Native women with these dolls. This should come as no surprise. The other Barbie dolls don't faithfully represent any other population either. Barbie is a fashion toy. She exists within her limits. Mattel is in a double bind. If they make a Native Barbie, they will get the details wrong; there are too many ways to be Native, and too few of them are easily reduced to representational clothing and a package blurb. If they don't make a Native doll, they are not representing a segment of the population. Either way they could be subject to critique. But whatever critical thinking suggests about the existence of such dolls, they are very successful. Ultimately Barbie is a good teaching tool because she has such dramatic brand recognition. All I have to do is mention Native American Barbie and the mind reels. What could such a thing be? I have no intention of demonizing Mattel or Barbie. I will not dwell on the absurdity of her variously notorious body parts, not even the visual strain of seeing high-heeled feet in moccasins and mukluks. I will not discuss the lack of any Native American Ken, though it does make me think that couples dancing at Barbie powwows must be a bit disappointing to some without him. No, I am more interested in what these dolls tell us about things that signify Indian-ness What visual cues make the Native Barbie dolls recognizable as Indian to the people who buy them? What are they wearing? How are they presented? And what does any of this indicate about perceptions of Native Americans?

There are ten Native American/American Indian Barbie dolls, one from each year since 1993 (the last doll was produced in 2003). Of the ten dolls, nine have black hair and one has very dark brown hair. They are all made of a medium brown plastic, the color varying slightly from doll to doll. Two of the dolls have their arms injection molded in "Hau" position: upper arm parallel to the ground, lower arm parallel to the body, hand open and facing away from the doll. This gesture should be familiar from Wild West films. The bodies are otherwise what one expects of a Barbie doll. A great deal of attention is paid to the clothes and the hair. As a fashion doll Barbie and accessories are geared in that direction. What does American Indian/Native American Barbie wear? All ten of the Indian Barbie dolls have fringe on their clothing. Nine of ten dolls have all or part of their hair in braids. Nine of ten wear jewelry. Eight of the ten dolls have seed beads somewhere on their outfit. Seven of them have feathers. Six of the dolls have headbands. Six of the dresses are made either entirely or in part of faux leather. Three of the dolls wear short faux leather shoes; the other seven wear boots. Many of these dolls come with additional equipment. The first Native American Barbie comes with a purse. Both American Indian Barbie dolls come with babies in carriers. Northwest Coast Native American Barbie has what is identified on the box as a Chilkat robe. Spirit of the Water Barbie has a rain stick. Spirit of the Sky Barbie carries both a dream catcher and a blanket. All but three dolls come with a brush. Every one of them comes with a stand. Looking over this list, my first urge is to assert that I reject this image of Indian women. It is important to keep in mind, however, that these dolls and widely available images similar to them are not intended to reflect us. They are intended to display the image of a Native woman, not the reality. As I slump in my home office barefoot, wearing thermal leggings and an oversized university sweatshirt, I view the dolls that are arranged around me on the floor with the same sense of curiosity that anyone would. What exotic lifestyle are these toys intended to represent? I sit here in front of my computer, fringeless, braidless, jewel and leather free, and try to decode them.

Every one of the special physical and clothing characteristics of these dolls should be familiar from conventional stereotypes about Indian women. Barbie herself is notorious for not looking like any real person, but aside from the standard deviations, nothing about these dolls is unexpected. What's more, these women, as is true for all Barbie dolls, are dressed up to do something. The two with babies are probably baby-sitting. The activities of the other dolls are more mysterious. None come with baskets, so they don't seem to be gathering anything. No one has tools of any kind. There are no musical instruments in evidence. They have no telephones, no roller skates, and no opera tickets. It is nearly impossible to guess what these characters are up to without a context. They are evidently engaged in cryptic Indian activities. Most of them have brushes so that they can be groomed. They are all supplied with stands so that whatever they are doing they can do it without the help of children's hands. The stands make me think of those dioramas in natural history museums. Papier-mâché or plastic human models are positioned as participating in ethnographically significant actions. Just like these diorama models, many of the Native Barbie dolls are permanently stuck in some or all of the clothes they are wearing. Headbands are affixed to the scalps with plastic staples; necklaces are too small to pull off without decapitation. A headband is a very specific accessory. Unless we are transforming Native Barbie into Summer of Love Barbie, it is a difficult item to incorporate into another outfit. It does not, for example, lend itself well to wear with a ball gown or an astronaut's uniform. Just by looking, the dolls with "Hau" arms have an even bigger problem. This would seem to be an enormous oversight in a fashion doll that is primarily about the clothes. One logical explanation suggests itself: These dolls are intended to be positioned and then left to be observed. They are, therefore, not up to much.

The context of Native American/American Indian Barbie is primarily a product of their boxes. We learn more about their lives through the text on the back. As any child could point out, Barbie boxes are usually a unique and instantly recognizable item. They are generally the specific Barbie rose pink, and the Barbie name appears prominently in the special Barbie font. The first three Native American Barbie doll boxes fit this model. The initial Native American Barbie was released in 1993 as a special edition. She came in a standard Barbie pink box. Written across the top of the box are the words "Inspired by the traditional dress of the first Americans!"[1] There is a stylized image of loomed beadwork running diagonally across the box. On the back there are images of a Plains war bonnet, a tepee, and a pair of barefoot, buckskin-clad children rolling a hoop toy with sticks. There is also this text:

> Hello! I'm Native American Barbie, part of a proud Indian heritage, rich in culture and tradition! Long ago, Native Americans each belonged to a *tribe*, a group of people who shared ancestors and customs. There were many different tribes, each with its own customs and dress. Some of us lived in *pueblos* (villages), slept in *teepees* (tents), and sewed clothes from *buckskins* (leather). We made many dishes with *maize* (corn), and were the first to dry strips of meat, which made *jerky*. For fun, children liked to play games of challenge, like wrestling and running, and rolling hoops with sticks! Native Americans relied on storytelling to bind them together. The eldest tribe member always passed on the ancient folk tales that kept the tribe's traditions alive. I'm wearing a traditional outfit, inspired by one of the tribes, with Indian artwork and beaded fringe, and soft leather *moccasins* (boots). Sometimes women wore braids, just like mine, and men wore fancy feather headdresses. We Native Americans of today still proudly keep alive the ways and wisdom of our ancestors, the first Americans. Good-bye![2]

The first thing that this writing establishes is the historical nature of Indian behavior. Notice that these traditions exist long ago. The very old pass on those ancient folk tales in order to "keep the tribe's traditions alive." Keeping the traditions alive is so urgent that it is mentioned again in the last bit of the blurb. The activities noted on the box are described as what Native people used to do. What also seems important to Native Barbie doll's world is pride. The word appears twice. Selected terms appeared on the box in bold type, which are then clarified in parentheses. To my understanding only two of these are in native languages. One is tepee, the classic default Indian house. The tepee is a standard Indian signifier. Moccasins, in this case defined as boots, are another standard bit of Indian paraphernalia. It is probably worth mentioning that these words are from two different Indian languages. The other words in boldface are interesting to me because to my understanding none of them are from Native languages. These are tribe, pueblos, buckskins, maize, and jerky. The image is simplistic, but the box also says that the doll is not intended for anyone under the age of three, so we should expect the simplicity. By implication, in 1993 the Mattel Corporation expected that even a three-year-old would recognize that Native people occupy an unspecific historical space in the United States. They keep their traditions alive through telling ancient folk tales. They are proud, and they eat corn and jerky. As for what this particular doll is doing, there is no real clue. Being part of a "proud Indian heritage" is not exactly an activity that would require a dress and boots. Perhaps keeping tradition alive is a relatively inert thing to do.

The next two Native American Barbie dolls follow the model of the first. They come in similar boxes with different printed beadwork patterns. Both the second and the third dolls of this series were reportedly going to powwows. From the third edition box we get:

> Hello from the *Southern Plains* of North America, which include Oklahoma and parts of Nebraska and Kansas. I'm getting ready for a genuine *Native American Powwow*, and you're invited to come join the fun! Long ago, the powwow began when one tribe wanted to form a friendship with another tribe. There was great feasting on roasted buffalo meat, corn, beans, and squash. It was also a time for gift giving. *The friendship bag*, a deerskin shoulder pouch decorated with porcupine quills, was packed with meat, tobacco, and other gifts, and presented as a symbol of friendship and goodwill. Today, tribes gather from all parts of North America for the powwow. A traditional feast is followed by friendly competition between tribes as they perform songs and dances from their past. I'll be leading *"The Round Dance,"* an age-old tribal dance performed in a circle while holding hands.

It originated in the *circle camps,* where *teepees* (cone-shaped tents) were pitched in a circle, leaving the center free for ceremonies. My dancing outfit is an updated version of a tribal princess costume. It's a mix of traditional style with the latest colors and accessories of today! I'll be pretty in my pink tunic and skirt with geometric patterns, white fringe, and ribbon trim. My *moccasins,* beaded necklace, turquoise earrings, and ring complete my modern-day powwow look! I've been looking forward to this celebration for so long! And now that you're here, it's sure to be extra special! Let the powwow begin![3]

These two dolls are going dancing at a powwow. In my personal experience a powwow is an endlessly complicated event that includes dancing, singing, eating, gossiping, and various other activities that help to both foster and create interpersonal relationships. Most first-time attendees find that the event is both more and less formalized than they expected. In the world of Indian signifiers, a real powwow would be far too complicated. Rather than argue the ways in which the Mattel description differs from my own experience, I would like to pull out the words and phrases that seem most common to me from contemporary mythology about Native people, the insistence that Barbie is preparing for a "genuine" powwow, for example. There is often an obsession with authenticity around anything Native. It is as though people expect to be fooled about Indian things. Perhaps this attitude is a holdover from snake oil salesmen. At any rate the use of the word *genuine* is curious because neither dress is anything I've seen worn at such an event. The rest of the text is less confusing. In this world of Indian symbols, it is not surprising to find corn, beans, squash, and roasted buffalo meat. I have never before heard of a "friendship bag," but the idea of symbolic gift giving is a familiar one. There seems to be some implication that there is just the one powwow. In the real world there is more than one every weekend from spring to fall. This, however, would not support the mythic image that Native people and everything about us is in the process of slipping into the past. The legend of the American Indian princess is one of the most striking of all Indian indicators. Many people report being related to one. The only sort of Indian princess that I am familiar with is a powwow princess. At some powwows they elect a princess based on dancing ability, decorum, regalia,[4] and other factors depending upon the powwow. This title is usually held for a year, and then someone else is elected. I believe that this practice is a fairly recent one, and I'm not aware of any historical costume that goes along with the title.

American Indian Barbie dolls, as distinct from Native American Barbie dolls, were released in 1996 and 1997. These dolls were part of the American Stories Collection, and each comes with a small storybook. Other dolls in the American Stories series include Pioneer Barbie, Civil War Nurse Barbie, and Patriot Barbie. The boxes for this series are larger than the usual Barbie box but are still the recognizable pink. The tagline for the American Stories Collection is "American History Comes to Life with Barbie!" Both of the Indian dolls in this series come with babies. They are the only dolls in the series that do. The lettering that says "American Indian" is crude. Each doll stands before an elaborately painted background. The 1996 edition is set in a Plains village with tepees and a stretching hide. The 1997 doll stands in a Southwest mesa scene with an eagle, a rabbit, buffalo, and a fox looking on. Each scene is very much in keeping with the storybook that is included with the dolls.

The 1996 book is titled *Baby Blue Feather*, which is also the name of the baby Barbie carries. Baby Blue Feather is Barbie's cousin. Their grandfather was the village storyteller, a task that now falls to Barbie. According to the little book, "Barbie lived on the great plains at the edge of a thick forest in the mid-west about the time the white men were building their first towns in the East."[5] When Baby Blue Feather gets sick Barbie worries. Then she gets a sign. A blue feather falls out of the sky onto her lap. She is inspired and tells a magic tale about a day when she was foraging for berries and met a magic bird. The bird had been shot with an arrow. After tending the injured bird with medicinal herbs, both Barbie and the bird sleep. When she awakes her baskets are full of berries and a blue feather lies on the top of one of the baskets. As she finishes her story, her aunt arrives carrying Baby Blue Feather, who is now cured of his illness. The 1997 Indian Barbie comes with a book called *Animal Gifts*. She is "known to her tribe as Running Springs, and her baby sister, Little Cloud."[6] This is the only reference to any of the Indian or Native Barbie dolls having a name other than Barbie. She too tells a magical story while she and her sister are out having a picnic of berries and dried meat. Hers is about how various animals help the tribe. These two dolls seem to have a great deal in common. They appear to indicate that among the things that signify Indian-ness are babies, berries, and some sort of vague magical connection to animals. The names are also interesting: Baby Blue Feather, Running Springs, and Little Cloud. These are exactly the sorts of names that Indian people are expected to have. Such names usually consist of a modifier and a noun. With the story series Mattel makes a distinction between Native American and American Indian. Both of the historical pieces seem to take place precontact, which would seem to imply that American Indian, for Mattel, is an older, more historical term than Native American.

The 1999 doll is unique to the series. Northwest Coast Native American Barbie is the only one of these dolls that has a discernible tribal affiliation. Northwest Coast Native American Barbie is Tlingit. Having a tribal affiliation lets this Barbie have a language as well. Each non-Native doll in the Dolls of the World collection begins her box explanation by greeting the reader in her language. Northwest Coast Barbie is the only Native doll that does that. "Yake'i ixw sateeni! (It's good to see you)."[7] The box is an irregular hexagon, in brown, with Barbie-version Tlingit decorative borders. Lying, as it is, on the floor of my office, it bears an unfortunate resemblance to my mental image of Sleeping Beauty's crystal coffin. The pictures on the back include a flying eagle, a collection of totem poles, and Northwest Coast Barbie clapping along to a trio of drummers. The important, boldface words on this box are: Sitka Spruce, bald eagles, Totem pole people, potlatches, Chilkat Robe, Winter Ceremonials, and the greeting and sign-off in Tlingit. Winter Ceremonials are described as "where we sing and dance, feeling close to the spirits of nature, as our ancestors did." Once again we describe Indian people as having a relationship with mythical nature based on ceremony. Toward the bottom of the box there are images of "Beautiful Barbie dolls representing 3 different countries!" The dolls are Spanish, Northwest Coast Native American, and Swedish. The Spanish doll is clearly from Spain. The Swedish doll is from Sweden. Why isn't Northwest Coast Native American Barbie called Tlingit Barbie?

Spirit of the Water is one of three dolls in a series undertaken in collaboration with Toys 'R' Us. Her box, an unusual one for a Barbie, is turquoise blue. The words "Limited Edition" are inscribed across the top of the box in French, Spanish, and English. There are rather subtle pseudo-petroglyphs depicting a deer, a fish, a turtle, a buffalo, a quail, and what I assume is a corn plant on either side of the Barbie logo. She herself stands in front of an abstract background. From the front there is no narrative, no indication of what this doll is up to, why she is dressed the way she is, or why she is holding a rain stick. On the back, again in English, Spanish, and French, is this copy:

> Beneath brilliant blue skies, a Native American woman dances, calling forth the great spirit. Centuries of tradition bring the promise that water will fall again upon the ancient lands and bestow a fruitful harvest. Now, clouds gather above, darkening the landscape to a soft dove grey. As precious raindrops fall, the beautiful woman celebrates the circle of life. Her "rainstick" answers the rhythm of the rain, its delicate music joyful as the wonder of nature. The splendor of nature and the glory of a proud culture are reflected in Spirit of the Water Barbie doll, an exquisite tribute to Indian heritage.[8]

Somewhere along the line Barbie learned to do a rain dance. Clearly this sort of thing has an audience. If it didn't sell, it wouldn't exist. This kind of text confirms something that I experience as an Indian woman and a teacher of American Indian Studies: It is impossible to overestimate the degree to which many people believe in inherent Indian mysticism. This mysticism seems to require exotic props, in this case a rain stick. The practice of this mysticism exists in a timeless and otherworldly space only available to the average person in glimpses through movies, books, and apparently the ownership of certain dolls. There are three dolls in this series. They were all released in Limited Editions.[9] The other two, Spirit of the Earth Barbie and Spirit of the Sky Barbie, each have equally dramatic texts. Spirit of the Earth Barbie, the first in the Spirit series, is housed in a brown box and is taking a walk through "the sacred land that has sustained her people for centuries. A generous bounty, the rich soil quietly shares its hidden mysteries."[10] On her box the words *mystery* and *harmony* each appear twice; other words that come into play are *sacred, reverent, power,* and *tradition.* Although Spirit of the Earth has no exotic prop, she is clearly participating in some sort of mystical communion with nature. The final doll in the series to date is Spirit of the Sky Barbie in a beige box. She is carrying a dream catcher. Her box says that she is watching horses race the wind and explains that "Spirit of the Sky Barbie doll captures the powerful magic and proud heritage of a Native American woman."[11] Proud, magic, heritage . . . capture, it's like a chant in itself and it becomes so familiar.

There is, by definition, an essential conflict for a Dolls of the World collection that contains Native examples. If these are dolls of the world, the world being here defined as external to the United States, where do these cultures come from? It isn't surprising that Native people are spoken about in the past. How can they really be both here and contemporary when they are made to seem so alien and exotic? We are unlikely to see Native Barbie in jeans, cowboy boots, and a powwow T-shirt because that would take away her otherworldly cachet. Native Barbie can't be here and contemporary without being dressed for a generally unfamiliar event. She can't really be wearing a contemporary powwow outfit because many of the items would seem too prosaic and once again pull her out of her exotic identity. A lawn chair and mirrored sunglasses simply don't scan as part of a proud and magical heritage. If they made her that way, she wouldn't sell. Each of these dolls is part of a story. It isn't a Native story. Native Barbie is just a character in the process of identifying, by exclusion, what is regular Barbie. Each Native doll since 1993 has become more iconic than the last. The Spirit series is the latest and is most affected by image rather than substance. They are the least undressable, the most mystical, the most expensive, and as Limited Editions there were fewer of them made. Native Barbie is, as the mythology goes with actual Indian people, dying out. I suppose it doesn't come as much of a shock. Without Native Ken it was only a matter of time before decline set in.

I try to approach this sort of thing with humor and patience rather than the indignation that is so much easier to feel in the face of this sort of use of our community's image. As usual my children help out; they reflect a new generation of activists. For several weeks I've had my typing area strewn with dolls and boxes and wadded bits of paper. During one particularly intense evening, my eldest made his way into my office. He read the box for Third Edition Native American Barbie. I heard him snort and go back downstairs. About half an hour later he returned with an old toy truck, a Barbie-sized ceramic mug, and a similarly sized coffee flask. He then arranged the doll in the truck with the mug and flask. When he noticed that I was watching, my teenaged veteran of four years on a powwow drum explained, "So she doesn't have to wait a year for the next powwow. When you get off the computer I'll look up driving instructions for next weekend on the Internet." He flashed me a grin and went away. A short time later my daughter came in. She read over my shoulder for a few moments and then went to the doll in the truck. "What dance style is she dressed for?" I shrugged. She stared at the doll for a few moments and then went away. About an hour later, she and my younger son came in with paper and pencils. They surrounded the doll and spoke together in serious and hushed tones. Plans were drawn up. After dinner that evening the two of them appeared again carrying a dance shawl. My girl had decided that the dress was most convertible to a fancy shawl outfit. My younger son made the shawl. My kids were unwilling to let Native Barbie exist outside of our community if she was going to live inside of our house. Taking matters into their own hands, they have corrected the problem. One day I fully expect to find her sitting in a lawn chair on my rug, listening to a tape of my oldest son singing, truck full of powwow flyers and Internet maps.

Notes

Hau is the word for hello in the Lakota language.
1. Mattel, Native American Barbie, 1992.
2. Mattel, Native American Barbie, 1992.
3. Mattel, Native American Barbie, 1994.
4. Regalia is the most accepted term for a dance outfit.
5. Kathryn Smithen, *Baby Blue Feather*, Mattel, 1995.
6. Agnes Davies, *Animal Gifts*, Mattel, 1996.
7. Mattel, Northwest Coast Native American Barbie, 1999.
8. Mattel, Spirit of the Water Barbie, 2002.
9. A limited edition consists of fewer than 35,000 dolls.
10. Mattel, Spirit of the Earth Barbie, 2001.
11. Mattel, Spirit of the Sky Barbie, 2003.

3

Liquor Moccasins

Philip Klasky

Americans have always had a robust interest in Native American kitsch, from brown-skinned Barbie dolls with Anglo features dressed in a strange mix of faux regalia to stucco tepee motels. Dream catchers shimmering with plastic beads are sold at national parks that inhabit the homeland of displaced aboriginal peoples. At curio shops you can buy drums adorned with air-brushed images of stoic, dark longhaired men and bare-breasted maidens; war bonnets with painted red feathers; plastic spears with flaccid rubber tips; and porcelain figurines of a slumped warrior riding off toward oblivion. This attraction to caricature is accompanied by a profound ignorance of the authentic. In fact, one begets the other as reality (and history) is eclipsed by a denial of the American Indian experience. The lack of understanding is a main ingredient of romantic views that seek to tame the truth and simplify the past.

On a recent trip to southern Utah to conduct ethnographic recordings of a Southern Paiute elder sharing about her boarding school experiences, Melissa Nelson and I flew into Las Vegas and rented a car for the trip to the Kaibab Indian Reservation. We drove down the Strip at night, bug-eyed at the theme casinos, monumental waste, and adult fantasy world of easy money, shabby glamour, and vicarious sex.

At the east end of the Strip, there is a novelty store with a marquee announcing, "Liquor Moccasins, Indian Jewelry 1/2 Off." Sometimes stray juxtaposition can be quite revelatory. In any case, it was just too good to pass up so we stopped to take a picture of the sign, and then, giving in to equal parts of curiosity and anthro-

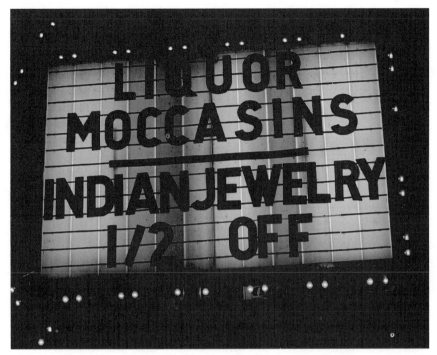

Figure 3.1. Native American Doll Shop, Las Vegas, Nevada.

pology, we entered the store armed with a digital camera. What we found exceeded both our fears and expectations. Hundreds of Indian dolls were displayed throughout the store—large and small dolls, males, females, and children, arranged on top of glass counters of taxidermy rattlesnakes and scorpions imprisoned in resin. The dolls' costumes consisted of someone's idea of Indian dress—lots of animal skins, feathers and furs, bells, beads, and war paint in every possible combination.

The shoe section sold cheap leather moccasins of all shapes and sizes, and the walls and shelves were covered in shields, dream catchers, lances, painted cow skulls, bows and arrows, and drums next to framed photos of Elvis, John Wayne, and Marilyn Monroe. Display cases of tacky jewelry could be had for half the price.

One section of the shop adorned with throbbing neon lights was dedicated to the sale of alcohol, an abundant commodity in the gambling town. We left the store with a camera full of images and escaped from Vegas.

I don't want to overanalyze (especially in an academic work), but I see the attraction to the phony artifact and cute Indian doll thing as akin to paving over the nature to avoid coming to terms with our relationship to it. We make what we fear or don't understand abhorrent or controllable, and make attempts to deal with the identity and substance of Native Peoples by possessing them in a diminutive form we can freeze and display. But there are other kinds of appropriation that are more serious and disturbing and deserve to be unearthed. We've seen the Jeep Cherokees and Apache helicopters, but did you ever hear about nuclear blasts with Indian names?

In a recent exhibit entitled "100 Suns," San Francisco photographer Michael Light culled archival photographs of atmospheric nuclear weapons testing and presented them simply with their code names, yield, location, and date of the explosion.

Among the spectacular and haunting images are "APACHE 1.85 megatons Enewetak Atoll 1956," "CHEROKEE 3.8 megatons Bikini Atoll 1956," "ZUNI 3.5 megatons Bikini Atoll 1956," "MOHAWK 360 kilotons Enewetak Atoll 1956," "SEMINOLE 13.7 kilotons Enewetak Atoll 1956," and "AZTEC 410 kilotons Christmas Island 1962."

Over the last sixty years the U.S. government has exploded over 1,000 nuclear weapons above and below the ground to determine their power and reliability. The first nuclear weapon tested exploded on the Apache Nation at the White Sands military reservation in New Mexico in 1945. Subsequent tests were visited upon aboriginal lands in the South Pacific. The Nevada Nuclear Weapons Test Site, only sixty-three miles from Las Vegas, is located in a vast area inhabited by the Western Shoshone before contact and ceded to them in the Treaty of Ruby Valley in the nineteenth century. The military and the Department of Energy have exploded over 800 nuclear devices at the site.

Toxic colonialism is not restricted to weapons testing. The Department of Energy has been trying to site a permanent high-level nuclear waste dump on the Mescalero Apache Indian Reservation in New Mexico, offering bribes and dividing the community in the process. Another dump hosting the poison fire from the inferno of nuclear power reactors has been proposed for the Goshute Indian Reservation in Utah, and President George W. Bush and Energy Secretary Abraham recently sold Congress on a high-

Figure 3.2. The Costs of Nuclear Testing.

level nuclear waste dump at Yucca Mountain on Western Shoshone land in Nevada.

The term "savages" has been applied to American Indians by the dominant culture because of their deep fear of the people they encountered as they marched across the country and because of the fierceness with which some Native Peoples have defended their lands and families. But the premeditated development and use of weapons that can kill hundreds of thousands if not millions of people in a single blast can only be described as savagery. Over 260,000 people were killed by the bombs dropped on the civilian targets of Hiroshima and Nagasaki. By naming their tests after Indian tribes, the bomb makers have tried to identify with a kind of primal power in a grotesque way.

There is more at play here than a policy of environmental racism that targets the disenfranchised. The sacred is desecrated by the profane fascination with destruction. In my view, using indigenous icons in this way is an attempt to counter the raw and mysterious spiritual force associated with Native cultures with destructive devices designed to obliterate the memory and guilt of a history of genocide, while asserting a dominance over the living as well as the dead.

4

(Dis)Locating Spiritual Knowledge: Embodied Ideologies, Social Landscapes, and the Power of the Neoshamanic *Other*

Sara C. Sutler-Cohen

Coming to the decision to be a shaman for a person who is not indigenous is complicated at the most basic level. Many people consider traditional healing for indigenous people a responsibility and a privilege—something you're born into, and not something you would choose for yourself. One of the more important aspects of "becoming" a shaman is to experience a liminal space of death (*metadeath*) where the shaman travels to other "worlds" to bring back knowledge reached only within the space of death. Within this liminal space their communities recognize the shaman as such. To carry the healing rites and stories of generations upon generations of ancestors is a feat, to say the least. What do you do when you're not born into an indigenous culture, yet you want to seek an altered cosmological set of knowledge?

For many nonindigenous people in the United States and Europe, the choice has become readily available, albeit for a cost. While often prohibitive, one can, for a fee, become a certified shaman, trained in the so-called Old Ways, and begin a career in healing to create a better world. While this sounds difficult at best, it has become the reality for thousands of people in the United States.

What is interesting to note is that there seems to be a rupture in identity for neoshamans. While the flyers and advertisements state that a workshop leader is a shaman, once in the workshop you are told by the leader that he or she is not a shaman. To wit, during my stint as a participant at a basic training shaman workshop, we were told that no one could tell us we were shamans. We could not claim we were shamans. Only "Spirit" could give us this information, so the role of the imaginary takes on a whole new realm of understanding with its own sets of knowledge.

In relation to space and home, these varied and created moments of self-actualization where interested parties can imagine "Spirit" speaking to them through dreams or dream *states* are of the utmost importance. Being able to recognize and call to "Spirit" during a workshop where would-be shamans are asked to mediate from one world to another is essential, thereby encouraging the creation of a sense of shamanic self via the imagination. In a sense, this can be construed as a way in which to reinscribe the construction of the narrative-as-justification of experience, and hence, justification of neoshamanic worth.

The fictional narrative is yet another venue in which neoshamanism is cropping up. I recently read a self-described "business fable" by Richard Whitely (2002), which tells the story of a CEO named Leon King who desperately tries to keep afloat his flailing midsize company, PRIMETEC. In *The Corporate Shaman: A Business Fable,* Whiteley makes it no secret that his life mirrors that of Jason Hand, the story's shamanic hero.

The concept of corporate shamanism is not a new one, and is clearly a growth industry, if the Whiteley Group is any indication. Richard Whiteley, who's had a healing office in Boston since the mid-1980s, has as his life goal to promote "healing in companies and 'enhanc(e)' the organizations' spirit or soul" (2002).[1] He is an award-winning and best-selling author whose most recent publication, *The Corporate Shaman,* has skyrocketed his entrepreneurial status and popularity as a speaker and healer of the misanthropic corporate culture of today. As a "spiritual consultant," Whiteley is among a growing community of concerned citizens passionately interested in rearranging from within the way in which companies conduct business. As with other corporate consultants, Whiteley stands to gain a hefty stipend at each of his speaking engagements.

Like his character Jason Hand, Richard Whiteley is a corporate shaman, which I would couch within the term *neoshaman*. Whiteley is a spearheading corporate consultant who has amassed astonishing global popularity among CEOs and the like who seek to find, heal, and deliver the so-called spirit back to their suffering corporations. His dossier is impressive, having been endorsed by Michael Harner (1982) and Deepak Chopra (2003) in addition to the CEOs of AT&T, Kodak, Southwest Airlines, and Mercedes Benz (Whiteley Group promotional packet, 2003).

In the area of neoshamanism, I am interested in two things. First, the degree to which corporate neoshamans engage in their own brand of advanced capitalist behavior, affording them the rights and privileges to spend their careers proclaiming the name of "teacher" in order to assist desperate professionals on their shamanic journeys,[2] and second, the degree to which cultural appropriation may come into play.

This capitalist project of neoshamanism seems like another incarnation of a historical moment where we see the possibilities of the political forces of hegemony inserting themselves into and alongside indigenous peoples in order to create what is represented as sharing, but what ultimately develops into the commodification of the *other*. The issue of control and spirituality is connected quite clearly because by selling shamanism as authentic worth, there is a creation of a sense of control via self-mandated leadership roles in the communities where neoshamanism is being lived out. Thus, religious and personal mastery become one and the same, and there is an elevated sense of control of the self within a set of beliefs in this particular set of cosmologies.

I would argue that this culture of advanced capitalism produces in the self a state of anomie wherein the so-called spiritual void starves for a connection to alternative sets of community life. In today's popular culture–driven political climate, we have a heightened sense of awareness of the self, regardless of where and/or how it is constructed and/or formulated. The contemporary crisis over meaning, and the way in which such crises are represented in popular culture, push for a constant hunt for the big individualist question of "Who am I?" The absorption of the other, in this case indigenous healers, supersedes the aforementioned question with "Who would I like to be?"

Among many theorists interested in studying religions, there is at least an agreement that for all religious/spiritual practices, including the New Age and neoshamanism, the larger-than-life questions are at the root of the need to believe: the meaning of life, the meaning of death, life after death/reincarnation, communication with the dead, the importance of religion shaping ethical decisions, and explanations of evil, disappointment, daily frustrations, and so forth. Further, the common thread among nearly all New Age groups, and subsequently neoshamanism, is that the root of New Age systems of belief demands a contestation of one's religious positionality (Brown 1997, Heelas 1996, and Lau 2000). That is to say, although many New Age practitioners/participants come from all walks of religious life, most coming *to* neoshamanism and embracing it come *from* a religion rooted in Christianity or Judaism, further differentiated by various sects.

Cultural studies scholar Kimberly Lau explains that the purpose of engaging in New Age theosophies is to connect with "an Edenic past when people lived in harmony with nature and with each other" (2000: 7). Thus, engaging in New Age spiritual practices is a logical approach to their overall spiritual unease. Along with this "void" comes the need for a physical incorporation of ideologies as they are interpreted by New Agers who wish to present in the physical form, indigenous spirituality. It is within this action of physical incorporation that the self absorbs the other.

In this particular moment, there is a concern with not only absorption, in creating a sense of self through the other, but also this idea that with the collection of material goods somehow representative of shamanism, one will also *become*. The concern is with the object (rattle, drum, rocks, beads, crystals, candles and fire, music) and not so much with its meaning.

The position of religious leaders is relevant here because of the way in which neoshamans use their rhetoric to advertise their teachings. People engaged in the neoshamanic movement often reflect on their spiritual void relative to others around them. Skyhawk Ojala, interviewed in the documentary *White Shamans Plastic Medicine Men* (Native Voices Public Television 1995), expresses her disappointment all through life with Christianity, until the "Great Spirit" spoke to her in a dream. "This is my cathedral," she passionately delivers to the camera as she waves her hand across the redwoods. "This is my church" (1995). Religious positionality also gives way to thinking about oneself against the backdrop of the other, in this case, indigenous shamans or medicine people. Ojala was looking for *something else*, and in that spiritual void also sat firmly the big questions.

This *void* has been part of the narrative discourse around alternative spiritual frameworks since the early years of New Age spirituality, as Philip Deloria (1998) discusses in his seminal work, *Playing Indian*, where he describes this condition of life quite aptly:

> In the 1960s and early 1970s, many Americans found themselves asking a new question: What is the meaning of meaning? Suppose truth had simply dried up and blown away in the blasting wind of nuclear anxiety, cultural relativism, and psychological self-reflexiveness? What if, as the Beatles had suggested, the world is like Strawberry Fields, a mystical, drug-hazy place where "nothing is real"? (156)

If this was true for the times, and certainly popular-culture texts have indicated as such with Timothy Leary's rhetoric, "Tune in, turn on, drop out," then it should be no surprise that the "Founding Fathers" (New Age Movements at the onset were overwhelmingly male-centered but with a peculiar bent toward the feminine Mother Earth) of New Age spiritual movements in the 1960s developed their spiritual expression out of a benign (and at times malignant) neglect of their own nonindigenous spiritual roots.

For these young people of the 1960s, the use of mind-altering drugs and the rise of political musical heroes were the beginnings of a demand for explanations other than what their traditional religions could provide for them. Thus began several dabblings in belief systems of "the other," that is, primarily at least in the Eastern-rooted religions such as variants on Buddhism, and including such "new" practices as yoga and meditation. Where people feel a spiritual void, there comes a "drive for bodily—and thus, personal, social, and planetary—transformations" (Lau 2000: 4).

The neoshaman dependent on the hard sell is *also* dependent on the spiritual void expressed by so many interested participants and followers. Stated earlier, the void comes out in the feeling that their root religions do not have all of, or even part of, the big answers to the big questions. On an online listserv group that I joined four years ago, I found several members who would express this. The following excerpts illustrate both the fascination with indigenous spirituality and the relative disappointment with their traditional religions:

> Sometimes I mourn for man . . . who have so lost their way somewhere . . . or maybe knew what was going on with the exception of a few. When I left the church I knew things were going on and religion had no answer for me. I researched and researched and found there were others who felt this same thing that I did . . . with little differences to it. (December 2001)

> I have been trying to find my way back to spirituality. (been adrift a bit . . .) I found a couple poems on the internet re: crows, wolfs, etc. and felt my heart filling with excitement and knowing. The crow poem was about how the person left his/her body and went up into the waiting arms which [*sic*] pulled him up to the voice of the crow, being held as securely as a newborn being cradled. Crows speak to me too and once I left my body as a crow and flew to a cave and found a lost part of my self and brought her back . . . was transformative for me. Sometimes I pray to Shaman's spirit for guidance. . . . (October 2001)

What has become clear from much of the neoshamanic literature (Harner 1982, McGaa 1990, Medicine Eagle 1991 and 2000, Villoldo 2000) is that for now, at least two generations of people starve for a spiritual connection, and indigenous people have a supposed vast wisdom, a spiritual system of belief that is all but lost to most people of late modernity.

Interestingly, neoshamans operate out of a place of spiritual descendancy, with nary an admission of colonial descendancy. What is often uttered in defense of their status as a leader or follower is "I was an Indian in a previous life" (Native Voices Public Television 1995). They emphasize healing through personal transformation as an individual's life project, or life course, and offer a promise that by transforming the self, the rest of "the people" will follow and be in balance and in harmony with the earth. Like Michael Harner's claim to have ingested Ayahuasca, the neoshaman need only to claim to have been "there," wherever "there" is, even when it is in a previous life. Neoshamans and other New Age practitioners are often acutely aware of a supposed lack of spiritual connection—and once found, there is a recognition that the modern world is cut off from its spiritual roots. What then occurs, however, is the taking up of indigenous systems of belief and the professing of a connection to Native ancestry or previous life claims.

Patenting Indigeneity: Capitalist Shamanism/Shamanic Capitalism

The conditions of possibility for neoshamanism are predicated on the virtues and realities of capitalism. Neoshamanism is dependent on capitalist ventures for survival. The capitalist tendencies of neoshamans, or of those self-described leaders of the New Age, drive and support the global moral project of shamanism, while rooted in these "authentic" indigenous cosmologies, the most accessible one being the connection to the earth. What grew out of the beatnik and deep ecology movements of the 1950s and the hippy movement of the 1960s is now a national trend for world peace via a spiritual connection to the earth, the conduit being that which is thought of as the authentic spiritual beliefs of the consumer.

A connection to an Edenic past often gives credentials to the neoshaman who then offers teachings and workshops for an inflated price. For example, Carol Proudfoot-Eagle and Sandra Ingerman of Santa Cruz offer a retreat entitled "Exploring Different Ways of Journeying and Ecstatic Experiences (Renewing Our Path and Our Circles): A Shamanic Retreat" each summer. The price (sans meals) is $620.00. The Basic Training Program in Shamanic Journeying (two 8-hour days) offered by Michael Harner and the Foundation for Shamanic Studies is $225. Mark Allen and Brant Secunda's Sport and Spirit retreat in Santa Cruz costs $275 with a nonrefundable deposit of $95, and Secunda's Hawaiian retreat, "Huichol Shamanism: Explore the Healing Way of the Heart," four days of "healing in Paradise," is a whopping $1,450 with a required nonrefundable deposit of $500. No scholarships are offered for any of these retreats. This neoshamanic work follows what Philip Deloria (1998) lays out in his work as a *fascination* many people have of "all things indigenous"; we now see the rise of these peculiar series of capitalist ventures, which result in the overwhelming move to patent and copyright indigenous ways practiced by nonindigenous people.

This individualistic approach to healing the mind, body, and spirit is an issue that scholars of New Age spirituality and neoshamanism investigate. In some contemporary scholarly writings on the potential fall of the power (social, political, and cultural) that organized, dominant religion will have over its followers, there is no indication that an *individual* approach to creating "wholeness" of the self and "oneness" with the (Mother) earth in spirituality is on the wane; on the contrary, since the 1990s, there has been a general growth in New Age practices (Lau 2000). This is most prominently evidenced in popular culture, if the successes of "Miss Cleo," LaToya Jackson, and the Psychic Friends Network (supported by Dionne Warwick), who feed on a spiritually empty-belly syndrome so many people seem to be afflicted with, are any indication.

Further, there is a fascination with the physical incorporation and ultimate embodied absorption of indigenous people. The following selection from the listserv illustrates this:

> I am Shadow Walker, and was given my name early in my training by the shaman, who was my mentor. I . . . dress somewhat different than most people. First, I have very long hair, which I have been inform [*sic*] is out of style. I wear mostly Native American type clothing, because I am out of Cherokee descent. I always wear my medicine bag, always no matter where I go, even at work. I often wear a head band, and . . . have a very unusual walking stick with feather [*sic*] and things. (December 2001)

Embodying and Commodifying the Other

Focusing on the attraction of New Age spirituality, late modernity, and the development of self-actualization via existential embodiments of the "other" may be one of the root causes of the need for an alternative spirituality and the move away from traditional religions (Giddens 1991). The idea of an ontological framework with which to operate outside of one's existence and *into* the existence of the other helps to explain the self-help movements of the 1980s as well as illustrates the way in which the individuals participating in neoshamanism activate existentiality to connect with others.

Notably, neoshamanism, while it seemingly calls for collective responses, the teachings, the seminars, the healings are publicly sold to *individuals*. As dominant societies move continuously toward global capitalism, so too will individuality reflect alternative ways of spiritually knowing. Further, through the embodiment of alternative human possibilities, particularly those racial and ethnic groups living *outside* of the dominant capitalist paradigms, we have the neoshaman as physically attempting an embodiment of indigenous peoples.

Philip Deloria writes:

> Playing Indian . . . has been constantly re-imagined and acted out when Americans desire to have their cake and eat it too. Indians could be both civilized and indigenous. They could critique modernity and yet reap its benefits. They could revel in the creative pleasure of liberated meanings while still grasping for something fundamentally American. It should come as no surprise that the young men and women of the 1960s and 1970s— bent on destroying an orthodoxy tightly intertwined with the notion of truth and yet desperate for truth itself—followed their cultural ancestors in playing Indian to find reassuring identities in a world seemingly out of control. (1998: 157–158)

Kimberly Lau (2000) in her work *New Age Capitalism: Making Money East of Eden* states that

> implicit in the popular discourses . . . is the belief in personal transformation through alternative, non-Western paradigms of health and wellness. Through what Robert Cantwell calls a physical and sensory "ethnomimesis"—that is, the imitation of another culture's traditions and practices—the rhetoric of holistic living is both operationalized and internalized. (3)

For Lau, the concern in her work focuses on the capitalist endeavors of those self-appointed gurus who offer salvation through health and wellness programs rooted in Eastern philosophies, and the successes of this branch of the New Age movement is vast: "If you don't practice yoga or t'ai chi, you probably know someone who does" (Lau 2000: 3). Like the neo-Yogi, neoshamans also sell their products, knowledge, and experience, at a high price, via this "physical and sensory 'ethnomimesis'" that Lau describes. Links can be drawn throughout Lau's work describing various capitalist ventures that depend on the spiritually vacant for profit as the "teacher" professionally embodies the "other."

The way in which Lau discusses New Age capitalism is relevant here to the project of neoshamanism in that there is a distinct connection toward the healing of the soul to the emptying of the pocketbook. While this is also an issue of the cultural theft of the spirituality of indigenous peoples, what makes it distinct is the way in which the ideology behind rugged individualism places members in a position where their spirituality is measured by their wealth. In this case, their wealth includes the possession of what is thought to be authentic rattles, beads, drums (especially), CDs, flutes, feathers, and the experience(s) of attending shaman training workshops, sweat lodges, and rituals led by a variety of self-proclaimed shamans who can be regarded as charismatic leaders. Further, we can see the way in which neoshamanism is an example of cultural imperialism acted upon by members as well as "teachers."

According to Laurie Anne Whitt (1995), cultural imperialism

is a form of oppression exerted by a dominant society upon other cultures, and typically a source of economic profit . . . [that] secures and deepens the subordinate status of those cultures. In the case of indigenous cultures, it undermines their integrity and distinctiveness, assimilating them to the dominant culture by seizing and processing vital cultural resources, then remaking them in the image and marketplaces of the dominant culture. (3)

This translates well to explain white American views of ownership and property in *general*, and helps to understand neoshamanism as a movement with cult-like tendencies (accumulation of wealth that is experience and objects to prove rank in membership) and an individualist moral project bent on healing the planet and its inhabitants. Whitt (1995) states, "When the spiritual knowledge, rituals, and objects of historically subordinated cultures are transformed into commodities, economic and political power merge to produce cultural imperialism" (3). She notes further in this article that the intellectual property rights (IPR), which give way to the copyright of neoshamanism (usually for nonprofit status as in the Foundation for Shamanic Studies), further support cultural imperialism (1995). One self-proclaimed shaman professed his intention to patent the sweat lodge because, in his opinion, indigenous people "no longer know how to do it properly" (Whitt 1995: 2).

You Can Own Grandma's Songs

In order to succeed in the art of cultural theft *legally*, intellectual property must act as a tool for that knowledge which can no longer be attached to an existing group of people. This allows cultural imperialism to come to fruition when the power of the dominant culture is enabled by its government to purchase the knowledge of indigenous peoples who are perpetually underrepresented. Another way to think about this issue is to consider the way in which images and symbols of North American Indian peoples have been co-opted and unilaterally put into the marketplace, as is the case with sports mascots. Henceforth, neoshamans are quite suddenly and without apology able to capitalize on a practice, which nobody can supposedly "own." It is in this way that racialized privilege in this situation can offer up personal gains from property (cultural, intellectual, tangible) not created by the other, but as ideas, beliefs, or ideals captured *from* them.

It is my belief that "Westernized" religion in general has become a commodity almost ad hoc in North America. It is a potential moneymaking industry, and anyone can take part. What formulates out of commodified Christendom are several evangelical purists, claiming end-of-the-world salvation (such as Marshall Applewhite of Heaven's Gate). You can even become an ordained minister if you have Internet access and the right amount of paperwork (www.ulc .org [retrieved December 22, 1999]).[3] It should come as no surprise, then, when neoshamanic "teachers" encroach upon indigenous religious sovereignty, claim it as their own, and ignore the pleas from the greater Indian populations that this theft not continue. After all, dominant Western religion (Christianity and all its guises) is available for purchase; why not every belief system? Religion as a commodity relates to this dominant worldview of individuals who own "things." The neoshaman is concerned with presentation, rather than spiritual meaning. Henceforth, the religious aspects are seldom separable from the worldviews of individualism and material ownership.

This suggests that white privilege is set up in such a way that justification is not necessary, nor is it questioned. For those exercising their white privilege, American Indian spirituality is simply *available*, and there is, henceforth, no accountability because of the imbalance of power dynamics. It is a given that those in power are *entitled* to acquire and to own whatever they see as an "ownable" object. It is part of the dominant American culture. Ironic, though perhaps not so surprising, is the moment at which the tables are turned. While indigenous ideas and systems of beliefs are readily available, those natural resources seemingly belonging at once to everyone and no one, such as minerals, air, oil, and water (and their ingestible inhabitants) are no longer free and clear to the general public.

What is strange in regard to neoshamanism is this seemingly inherent assumption that there is some form of justifiable information exchange going on here, both on an individual level, as well as on a larger level, between indigenous healers and tribal members and members from the neoshamanic circles. Neoshamans proselytize their New Age shamanic systems of belief and practice (always referring to them as the "old ways") as individually based practices for personal gain. The indigenous spiritual leaders' practices, however, are not meant for the public market and not meant for public consumption. Most indigenous ways of practice, which indeed may acknowledge the self, specifically how the self relates to the greater community, further seek to connect with family, community, ancestry, and the Mother Earth.

While New Ageism is no stranger to purchasing the Mother Earth language of spirituality, it is often sold as a way for New Agers to *personally* connect with nature (Whitt 1995: 23). Hence, it is an internal effort for one to be closer to the earth and a prayer for the connection with all living things, the earth, the universe, and all that is considered sacred. It is in this moment that neoshamans are fully engaged in their community, however individual the path may be, to heal the earth through collective shamanic practice.

While the path to all things indeed involves lifted indigenous rhetoric, neoshamans and their followers/participants rarely, if ever, have any real contact with the groups from which their beliefs are derived. So while neoshamans proclaim a great respect for indigenous people, they ironically ignore the protests of indigenous communities at large. Neoshamanism, then, serves as a metaphor for a modern-day Doctrine of Discovery. Indian people, it seems, are human enough to possess a "beautiful" religion, yet too "savage" and nonconforming to legally protect them from cultural imperialism.

When neoshamans claim their "Indian names" came to them from the Creator (or whispers from the trees, from a raven, from a deer, from a bear, and/or from the sky; they "heard" them from a rock, in a dream, in a vision, or in a sweat), they are ignoring the process by which Indian people receive their names. Neoshamans are not legitimately given the names in the Indian way, but they are, to the New Ager, fully legitimate (and often trademarked). According to Indian activist Betty Cooper, "the Indian name comes from a very special place . . . the family name carrying on its traditions. Those are treated with great respect and honor" (Cooper, interviewed in *White Shamans and Plastic Medicine Men*, Native Voices Public Television 1995).

Many of these folks do not travel around the globe on a mission to heal the earth. Although many (like Cedar Woman) are available for rental, most stay put where they can be easily located for wealthy vacationers. The modus operandi of neoshamans is rooted in the "authentic" Native American philosophies that collectively represent this particular kind of capitalist encroachment upon indigenous people.

In closing, it is important to understand the notion of *internal sovereignty* as it serves to help give efficacy to the voice of indigenous tribal members and healers in terms of passionate arguments against the theft and commodification of indigenous spirituality.

> Sovereignty is the force that binds a community together and represents the will of a people to act together as a single entity. A sovereign community possesses certain rights, including the rights to structure its government as it desires, to conduct foreign relations and trade with other nations, to define its own membership, to make and enforce its own laws, and to regulate its resources and property. . . . Traditional Indian culture has made little distinction between the political and the religious worlds. (Deloria 1998)

Perhaps the final sentence here is the most important in terms of understanding the parameters of internal sovereignty for indigenous people. The very idea of internal sovereignty proclaims that indigenous people know who they are and where they come from on a deeply intense level. The fact that all realms of sovereignty are related to the way in which tribal governments have traditionally run is indicative of a worldview difference between indigenous and nonindigenous people. The United States, in its legal separation of church and state, cannot likely impress upon its people the disrespect the commodification of spirituality shows for indigenous people.

In their coauthored article, "On the Idea of the Indigenous" (1999), John Brown Childs and Guillermo Delgado-P critically examine the way in which indigenous people have been closely examined by anthropologists, historically and contemporarily, disputing a homogenous *idea* of *a* people.

> Most anthropologists . . . have handsomely benefited from their interactions with indigenous peoples, producing research that only in limited cases has been returned to native communities.
>
> In the Americas, the development of the term "indigenous" by and for the people to whom the term applies is itself but a chapter in a centuries-long story of resistance to colonial disruptions. (211)

It is much deeper than a simple explanation, as the authors suggest above. Internal sovereignty is a state of *being*, a state of knowing who you are, and clearly comes from the very *reality*, and not the *idea* of the indigenous. It is directly connected to a belief system belonging to indigenous peoples, and vice versa. For neoshamans to encroach upon indigenous spirituality is equal to attempting to fully and finally decimate the First Peoples of the Americas. To rob someone of their internal sovereignty is no different than asserting one's dominance over a subaltern and colonized group.

Neoshamans exercise their (white) privilege by exploiting American Indians and putting a price tag, via copyright laws, on spirituality. Further, it should be noted here that not only are neoshamans "sharing" their knowledge with others (that is, if one has the money to partake in the "sharing"), but also they are posing as spiritual teachers. For many Indian people, this is the ultimate dishonor and disrespect. One cannot *decide* to be a spiritual leader; rather, that gift must be passed down from the Elders, at times within the family, and usually within a tribe, and the most prominent role of that leader is the healing of his or her people, as seen within historical contexts. Of course, many Elders who are true spiritual leaders, medicine men and women, and/or shamans may indeed share with or affect others, including whites, showing a spiritual path of knowledge, but not for a price.

Some Final Thoughts

In attempting to understand the development of neoshamanism, it is important also to understand the development of the white imagination, which we can see reflected in popular-culture texts but also in the development of late modernity and the development and use of the Internet as a site for spiritual reflection and collective spiritual activism on the part of New Age participants. It is imperative to understand that so many curious individuals are not simply engaging in neoshamanism but are attempting to commodify it via developments in the corporate world, to bring in shamanic teachings to both small and large companies, as in the case of Richard Whitely, author of *The Corporate Shaman* (2002).

Neoshamanism, that sector of New Ageism professing to heal the earth via collective work of individual followers, hearkens back to nature but does so in a way that puts a price tag, a copyright, and a patent on the spiritualities of a diverse, yet distinct (and colonized) group of people. The danger here is rooted in the belief by many Indian people that their spirituality is the only thing they have left to call their own. It is that notion of internal sovereignty and (spiritual) dignity that is being encroached upon by "wanna-be" Indians, which serves to undermine indigenous spirituality. While neoshamans continue to romanticize indigenous ways of spiritual knowing and traditional culture in order to escape their own sense of cultural and spiritual destruction, they "pursue spiritual meaning and cultural identification through acts of purchase. Although New Agers identify as a countercultural group, their commercial actions mesh quite well with mainstream capitalism" (Aldred 2000: 1). Therefore, neoshamans and their followers/consumers are a seeming walking contradiction. Their "imagined community" of collective so-called shamanic virtues and practices to heal the earth in turn becomes a pit of despair in which faith and healing is only made available through the living, breathing culture of capitalism.

Notes

Sections of this paper were presented at the American Studies Association Meeting in Hartford, Connecticut, October 2003.

1. In addition to the Whiteley Group, there are others including, but not limited to, the Shamanic Vision Institute (www.shamanicvision.org), which also wants to "bring shamanic healing to the corporate community" (2003).

2. The "journey" is one of the more common aspects of neoshamanism that is used to train people interested in becoming authentic shamans and is done in nearly every workshop. In one of the training sessions I've been to, we "journeyed" six times in two days to the "lower" and "upper" worlds in order to get advice from power animals, plants, dirt, or people—dead, alive, or never having touched the planet Earth with the soles of their feet. "Journeying" consists of the "client" laying down on her back, arms at her side, head on a pillow, eyes closed while someone drums a beat of four to seven counts, repetitively, until the "client" can enter into a subconscious world whereby in her meditative state she is enabled to shoot through a visible hole (in a tree, the ground, a swimming pool, etc.) until she comes to a stop. There, she will wait for her power animal/shaman/plant/spirit helper to answer her question(s). At the drumming signal of seven short four-count beats, she is to return back the way she came.

3. This website boasts the following:

Welcome! You are about to become an ordained minister with the Universal Life Church, Modesto, California. Please be sure to find out about the legal doctrines governing your country, state, or province. After you fill out the following form, your request will be promptly reviewed by our pastoral staff. You will receive notification of your ordination status by email. Ordination ceremonies are performed several times each week, so normally you will hear from us within a day or two. *Please* be sure to include a valid email address with your application, so that we may notify you promptly. We do not furnish the names of our ministers to any outside organization. Please note that you MUST provide your full name and a mailing address. This information is required in order to maintain the integrity of the records, and will be guarded as a confidential record.

References

Aldred, Lisa. "Plastic Shamans and Astroturf Sun Dances: New Age Commercialization of Native American Spirituality." *American Indian Quarterly* 24, no. 3 (2000): 329–352.

Brown, Tom. *Way of the Scout: A Native American Path to Finding Spiritual Meaning in a Physical World*. New York: Berkley Books, 1997.

Brown Childs, John, and Guillermo Delgado-P. "On the Idea of the Indigenous." *Current Anthropology* 40, no. 2 (1999).

Chopra, Deepak. *Spontaneous Fulfillment of Desire: Harnessing the Infinite Power of Coincidence*. New York: Random House, 2003.

Cook-Lynn, Elizabeth. *Why I Can't Read Wallace Stegner and Other Essays: A Tribal Voice*. Madison: University of Wisconsin Press, 1996.

Deloria, Philip. *Playing Indian*. New Haven, CT: Yale University Press, 1998.

Deloria, Vine, Jr. *Spirit and Reason: The Vine Deloria, Jr., Reader*. Golden, CO: Fulcrum Publishing, 1999.

Fanon, Frantz. *The Wretched of the Earth*. New York: Grove Press, 1968.

Giddens, Anthony. *Modernity and Self-Identity: Self and Society in the Late Modern Age*. Stanford, CA: Stanford University Press, 1991.

Hammer, Olav. *Claiming Knowledge: Strategies of Epistemology from Theosophy to the New Age*. Boston: Brill, 2001.

Harner, Michael. *The Way of The Shaman*. New York: Bantam Books, 1982.

Heelas, Paul. *The New Age Movement: The Celebration of the Self and the Sacralization of Modernity*. Oxford: Blackwell, 1996.

Kehoe, Alice Beck. *Shamans and Religion: An Anthropological Exploration in Critical Thinking*. Prospect Heights, IL: Waveland, 2000.

Lau, Kimberly. *New Age Capitalism: Making Money East of Eden*. Philadelphia: University of Pennsylvania Press, 2000.

Lenin, V. I. *Imperialism: The Highest Stage of Capitalism, A Popular Outline*. New York: International Publishers, 1939.

McGaa, Ed. *Mother Earth Spirituality: Native American Paths to Healing Ourselves and Healing Our World*. San Francisco: HarperSanFrancisco, 1990.

Medicine Eagle, Brooke. *Buffalo Woman Comes Singing*. New York: Ballantine Books, 1991.

Memmi, Albert. *The Colonizer and the Colonized*. Boston: Beacon Press, 1967.

Native Voices Public Television. *White Shamans Plastic Medicine Men*. 1995.

Nkrumah, Kwame. *Neocolonialism: The Last Stage of Imperialism*. New York: International Publishers, 1965.

Said, Edward. *Culture and Imperialism*. New York: Vintage Books, 1993.

Seidman, Steven. *Contested Knowledge: Social Theory in the Postmodern Era*. Second ed. Malden, MA: Blackwell, 1998.

Shamanic Vision Institute. www.transcurrents.org/aboutsvi.htm.

Shamans Cave listserv. Online dialogues as ongoing research. Accessed November 2001–September 2003.

Stannard, David. *American Holocaust: The Conquest of the New World*. New York: Oxford University Press, 1992.

Sutler-Cohen, Sara C. "White Shamanism and the Commodification of American Indian Spirituality." Unpublished paper. Presented at the Pacific Sociological Association annual conference in March 2000, San Diego, California, and the Fourteenth Annual California Indian Conference in October 1999, San Luis Obispo, California.

Taussig, Michael. *Shamanism, Colonialism, and the Wild Man: A Study in Terror and Healing*. Chicago: University of Chicago Press, 1987.

Villoldo, Alberto. *Shaman, Healer, Sage: How to Heal Yourself and Others with the Energy Medicine of the Americas*. New York: Harmony, 2000.

Whiteley, Richard. *The Corporate Shaman: A Business Fable*. Philadelphia: HarperCollins, 2002.

Whitt, Laurie Anne. "Cultural Imperialism and the Marketing of Native America." *American Indian Culture and Research Journal* 19, no. 3 (1995).

5

Masks in the new Millennium

Winona LaDuke

> In the twenty first century, the battle to protect Indian land
> and culture has become even more complicated as it is
> now possible to steal Indian property, names, traditions,
> and symbols without ever setting foot in Indian country
> or coming in contact with the tribes or individual Indians
> from whom these pieces of cultural property are being
> stolen.[1]

They are the *Fighting Whites,* an intramural basketball team at the
University of Northern Colorado. A nearby Eaton High School (also
in Colorado) team—the Reds—uses a Native American caricature
for its logo and has, despite many requests, refused to change its
name. Eaton School District superintendent John Nuspi has maintained that the logo is not offensive and finds criticism insulting,
responding, "Their interpretations are an insult to our patrons and
blatantly inaccurate."[2]

Organized in early 2002, by both Native and non-Native students, the University of Northern Colorado team came up with
the "Fighting Whites" logo and slogan to have a little satirical fun
and to deliver a simple, sincere message about ethnic stereotyping.
Having had national press coverage on their logo, which features
a clean-cut white male in a business suit, and the slogan, "Every
thang's going to be all white," the Fighting Whites, including Ryan
White, John Messner, and Charles Cuny, are putting the profits of
their T-shirt sales toward scholarships for Native students.[3] "It's not
meant to be vicious, it is meant to be humorous," explains Ryan
White, a Mohawk who is on the team. "It puts people in our shoes,
and then we can say 'now you know how it is, and now you can
make a judgment.'"[4] An excellent response, one might say, to the

issue of Native mascots in the new millennium. And by the close of 2002, the group had raised over $100,000 in T-shirt profits, which they are now putting into scholarships for Native students.[5]

The doorway through which one observes the controversy over Native American mascots and commercial imagery is full of fog and fire. It is the fog and haze of the history of this country. It is a reminder of the icons of westward expansion, colonialism, and domination. It is also the fire of voices, hearts, and passions of those who have used the imagery to justify its creation, while those, "in whose honor"[6] the imagery is supposedly created, challenge its foundations. This struggle over representation is central to understanding the right of a people to determine their destiny, their imagery, and the use of their names. It is a struggle not on battlefields but rather one for the minds of Americans all across the United States.

A quarter of a century after Stanford University and Dartmouth College retired their Native American mascots, over six hundred separate educational institutions have joined them. In each case the institutions have transferred their loyalties from a Native-theme mascot to an animal or other creation, without, one could presume, huge psychological trauma.[7] There are at least eighty colleges and universities that still retain Native Americans as mascots, as well as hundreds of high schools. These institutions continue to refer to their school teams as the Redmen, the Warriors, the Indians, or some other presumed likeness to Native people.[8] Not only is the mascot and subsequent commercial imagery controversial, it is also symbolic not only of the struggles over Native identity but also of the battle over defining American history and what is remembered and retold, as well as what is omitted.

I have spoken many times at colleges and universities across the country on this issue. On numerous occasions, I have asked my audience to raise their hands and name at least ten distinct Native nations in North America. Whether they are doctors of law, architects, or college students, it is rare that I find more than a handful worthy of the task. Such is the amazing reality of an American education! While most of our children can name a set of superheroes into obscurity, or a list of sports teams, presidents, and supermodels, very few can name Native nations who have lived on this land for a millennium.

Even in our own shared territory, audiences struggle. I have asked businessmen in the town that adjoins my reservation if they could name ten different types of Native people, and surprisingly (or not so surprisingly) few were even able to name the indigenous nation in whose presence they lived, referring to them as "the Indians." This is a sad truth. American educational institutions have done a fairly poor job of teaching American history, particularly from the perspective of Native people. Little is known about the history of genocide in this country, or the democratic, medicinal, or agricultural foundations of this country, which originate in Native America. Even less is known about the history of the treaty-making period or the present struggles of Native people. By and large, most discussions of Native people take place in the past. In fact, whenever I have the occasion to ask people to name Native nations with whom they are familiar, invariably they are only able to produce the names of Native people from Westerns: the Comanches, the Navajo, the Sioux, the Cheyennes, the Crow, and so forth. Ask these same crowds to name famous Native women in history and two will appear—Pocahontas and Sacajawea, a rather limited foundation, and only those profiled most recently in Hollywood movies.

In the new millennium, the most prevalent imagery of Native people is derogatory. According to Dr. Cornel Pewewardy, a professor at the School of Education at the University of Kansas,

> In popular culture, using a person for your clown has always been one of the major ways to assert your dominance over a person or a group of people. Mockery becomes one of the more sophisticated forms of humiliation in sporting events. Therefore, clowning and buffoonery during ballgames became one of the primary ways in which Indian mascots are used as clowns while sports fans manipulate and keep in place negative images during school related events.[9]

It is in this context, along with the added context of trying to have an authentic Native identity in the era of MTV and the culture-eating elements of globalization,[10] that the discussion and struggle over Native American mascots and imagery are both urgent and pervasive. The prevalence of Disney, Coca-Cola, MTV, and commercial imagery have seeped largely through the mass media into the minds of many, even isolated indigenous cultures. As C. Richard

King and Charles Springwood write in *Team Spirits*, Native American mascots afford a

> splendid opportunity to explore the construction and contestation of particular versions of race, especially Indian-ness and whiteness; to highlight the colonial legacies and "post colonial" predicaments of American culture; and to outline a nuanced account of the changing position of Native Americans in American society from invented icons to embodied actors.[11]

The use of most Native American mascots involves some sort of "creation myth" retold by academic institutions themselves to justify and instill a mysterious wonder in the members of the community. When an academic institution is challenged to change the name, a number have responded by reiterating the legitimacy of the creation myth. These institutions typically begin by alluding that "although many other mascots are indeed racist," teams such as Illinois and Florida State, for instance, insist that their "Chiefs" (Illiniwek and Osceola) are not "mascots" but rather "symbolize the spirit of the Fighting Illini."[12] Such comments solicit support for particular local mascots, suggesting they exist in a semiotic vacuum, to be "read" as if they bore no trace of the conditions of possibility that motivated the widespread invention of Indian mascots. Of course, King and Springwood would write in *Team Spirits*, "the significance of any Native American representation, let alone an athletic mascot, cannot fully be appreciated if it is seen as historically unrelated, in systematic tandem with all other similar representations to the construction and maintenance of non-Indian imperial identities."[13]

The creation of mythic images for sports teams is an anomaly in itself. A particularly American adaptation and re-creation of the crests of ancient knights, mythic images are, as Roland Barthes, the French semiologist puts it, "ubiquitous."[14] They are "half amputated, they are deprived of memory, not of existence. They are at once stubborn, silently rooted there and garrulous, and speak wholly at the service of concept."[15] Charlene Teters, a Spokane woman who has been the lightning rod for the present-day mascot struggle, states that

> these caricatures and stereotypes are really intended as prisons of image. Inside each desperately grinning Cleveland Indian and each stoic Redskin, Brave, or Chief Illiniwek mascot, there is someone

we know. If you look hard enough and don't panic, you begin to see the eyes and the hearts of these despised relatives of ours, who have been forced to lock their spirits away from themselves and from us. I see our brothers and sisters, mothers and fathers captured and forced into images they did not devise, doing hard time for all of us. We can liberate them by understanding this, and ourselves.[16]

Not the Fighting Sioux: UND and Mascots

Somewhere amid all of this is the battle over a University of North Dakota hockey team called the "Fighting Sioux." It is a strange and twisted tale in which a neo-Nazi makes a large gift to a university, any semblance of morals and ethics are forgotten, and Native people find themselves, once again, at odds with a large university system. This strange story begins with Ralph Engelstad, who has sort of humble origins. The son of a salesman, Ralph was raised in Thief River Falls, Minnesota. At seventeen, he began his rather modest career by unloading boxcars in Grand Forks, but a professor at the University of North Dakota found he had been a goalie on the Thief River Falls hockey team and arranged for a scholarship. After a couple of "uneventful seasons," Ralph finally completed a degree in commerce and began a career as a building contractor. He then moved to Las Vegas in 1959 and got a pretty good chunk of change when he sold billionaire Howard Hughes 145 acres on which to build the North Las Vegas Airport. Ralph reinvested his money in the casino business, launching the Imperial Palace Casinos in Las Vegas and Biloxi, and later in the construction of the Las Vegas Motor Speedway, home of the NASCAR races.

It was the birthday parties that pushed Ralph's notoriety over the edge. In 1988, Nevada state regulatory authorities discovered that Ralph Engelstad held birthday parties for Adolf Hitler in a special room of Nazi memorabilia known as the War Room in his casino. The April 20 birthday parties in 1986 and 1988 featured, according to reporters, "a cake decorated with a swastika, German food and German marching music."[17] The Nevada Gaming Control Board found a plate used to print bumper stickers with the message "Hitler was Right," which were sent out from Engelstad's hotel. Ralph's embellishments and passion landed him a 1988 fine from the Nevada Gaming Control Board for $1.5 million for damaging the reputation of the state of Nevada.

It was about that same time that the University of North Dakota started to put the squeeze on its wealthiest alumnus, Ralph Engelstad. Concerned with possible problems as to Ralph's strange leanings, the university dispatched a delegation of seven representatives from the university to Las Vegas, to meet with Englestad and tour his facilities. At that time, Ralph had pledged a measly $5 million for the hockey stadium, but the fund-raising program knew more money was in the cards. The delegation was treated with the utmost hospitality by Engelstad, but some people were still concerned. English Professor Elizabeth Hampsten was shaken; paintings of naked women stood next to busts of Hitler wearing Mr. Engelstad's hat and, perhaps most nauseating, a Nazi propaganda poster depicting children staring out of windows on a train. The caption read "Summer Holiday," and as Elizabeth Hampsten recalls, "I knew the meaning . . . wasn't a summer holiday."[18]

The university panel came to a rather sorrowful conclusion that Ralph was not actually a Nazi sympathizer but had simply shown "bad taste." That cleared the way for the fund-raising program to put a bigger squeeze on Ralph for a $100 million "donation," dismissing Engelstad's interests as idiosyncratic. Although Hampsten had objected, she regrets that it was not "loudly enough."[19] Meanwhile, down in Las Vegas, Nevada, Ralph Englestad sits cozily in his room filled with his busts of Adolph Hitler, Hitler's 1939 Parade car and Heinrich Himmler's Mercedes, and a life-size portrait of Hitler, with the inscription "To Ralphie from Adolph" emblazoned upon it. He is a happy man, a smug man. Then came the problem with the name, the Fighting Sioux.

It is important to keep in mind that the University of North Dakota is a hockey powerhouse, viewing the world from its frozen corner of the prairie where outdoor hockey can be played for at least four months a year. The university prides itself in having sent at least fifty players to the National Hockey League. The team usually has a regular place in at least the semifinals of the "Frozen Four," the college hockey play-offs. Hockey is the stuff of life to some of the University of North Dakota's alumni. The short-lived name the "Flickertails," an earlier mascot, did not, it appears, summon up the powerful imagery and magic necessary for a powerful hockey team.

The opening of the Ralph Engelstad Hockey Arena compromised the university's integrity and has certainly put the issue of racism in sports in the limelight. The $100 million from Engelstad to the University of North Dakota was one of the ten largest "gifts" ever given to a public university, but it has put a focus on the true price of corporate and private contributions to our university system. It also summons a puzzling question: How can anything built by a man who dresses up in a Nazi outfit be an honor to Native people? In response, Native youth got involved in antiracism in sports activities following the opening of the new arena.

A small but mighty delegation of White Earth youth attended the October 2001 Racism in Sports conference at the University of North Dakota. It was the first demonstration for most of the kids from the White Earth Reservation. The Rice Lake boys had signs that read, "Indians are people, not mascots" and "Respect our Human Rights." A cheeky two-year-old from Round Lake had a sign that read, "Go Home Pilgrims," and another had a sign that read, "Hinkley Honkeys." Federal marshals, empowered to insure that our First Amendment rights were protected in a hostile environment, watched over the small demonstration of a hundred or so folks who stood in the bitter wind in the shadow of the immense Ralph Englestad Hockey Arena. Our voices were strong, but with a price tag in the hundreds of millions of dollars, Native students and those who support self-determination in the imagery of Native Americans did look like David in the face of Goliath.

The Fighting Sioux indeed! The name itself is sort of the antithesis of the state of North Dakota. The state has engulfed five reservations: Turtle Mountain (Anishinaabe), Spirit Lake (Dakota, also known as the Ft. Totten Reservation), Sisseton/Whapeton (Dakota), Standing Rock (Lakota), and Fort Berthold (Mandan, Hidatsa, and Arikara). The fact that three of the reservations have names that are left over from the Indian Wars and the forts pushed into the hearts of Indian territory to "tame the hostiles" should be a small indicator of the conflict between settler and Native. Twenty years after the assassination of Little Crow, the army had been given control of the Indian reservations in North Dakota and elsewhere. From these places, like Fort Yates, the ultimate assassination of a great chief like Sitting Bull would take place.[20] Indeed, it was from Fort Abraham Lincoln, just south of present-day Bismarck, North Dakota, that General George Armstrong Custer left for the Battle of the Little Big Horn. As the saying goes, he instructed the Indian agents at the Fort "not to do anything until I get back," and yet they are still waiting.[21]

The state of North Dakota continues to battle for its existence. Demographically, the state is affected by a net annual loss in population, with particular reference to non-Native people: 62 percent of the state has returned to frontier status, as farms dwindle and populations move out. Native communities, on the other side, seem to be increasing dramatically in population. The climate and landscape was really intended for buffalo, not for farming, hence some of the challenge to the state's economy. Then there is the military. With the Cold War came the "dew line"—the creation of a string of military bases that could both defend the United States against the Soviet threat and attack as needed. With the Cold War buildup and nuclear weapons proliferation, it is said that the Lakota Nation itself (circumscribed by the 1868 treaty) constitutes the third greatest nuclear weapons power on the face of the earth. North Dakota constitutes a lion's share of that power.[22]

The military base at Grand Forks remains as one of the only economic boons for the region, with 7,500 or so residents. As the Native students struggle under piles of books at the University of North Dakota School of Medicine (or some of the twenty-five other primarily Native programs that have attracted the 350 Native students to the school in Grand Forks), they are faced with a strange irony on a campus of 11,000. Most feel like they are being spit on every day. They are still sporadically called "prairie niggers," accused of living off the government dole, and termed "crybabies," as if they are unappreciative of the presumed largesse of the University of North Dakota. The university and graduate school are already tough for most people, let alone going to school in a town torn over the issue of race, yet comfortable enough in bedazzling itself with the money of racists.

Racism in the northern United States is no doubt subtle. Scott Nelson, past sports editor for the University of North Dakota Student paper, told a reporter for the *Chronicle of Higher Education*,

"There are no hate crimes. It's not like the Deep South in the '60s. And, it is the strange irony, in which thousands of students 'will wear a jacket,' explains Nelson, 'with a mascot of an Indian, but won't talk to one.'"[23]

That is why, in the midst of this irony, the University of North Dakota's claim that the Fighting Sioux logo is an honor to Native students comes across as an insult to many. Furthermore, a hockey arena emblazoned not only with the Sioux logo, but with a huge statue of Sitting Bull is strange and troubling to the Standing Rock Sioux Tribe. All this "honoring" was done despite the written opposition of the Standing Rock Sioux Tribe, which objected to the statue and joined with every other Tribal Government in North Dakota to oppose the use of the name as a mascot.

It was in the fall of 1930 when the University of North Dakota decided to change its name from the Flickertails to the Fighting Sioux. The decision to change the name came about, it seems, because the "Flickertails" were not considered a formidable foe against the Mighty Bison, North Dakota State University's nickname and UND's longtime rival. Native journalist Holly Annis found an internal UND memo, discussing the merits of the name change:

1. "Sioux are a good exterminating agent for the Bison."
2. "They (Sioux) are warlike, of fine physique and bearing."
3. "The word Sioux is easily rhymed for yells and songs."[24]

There was little debate, and the team re-emerged with its new face. The first Native American students' group was formed at the University of North Dakota in 1969. The group called for the creation of a cultural center for Native students and an Indian studies program and an end to using the "Fighting Sioux" nickname and a mascot known as "Sammy the Sioux."[25]

The cultural center was created a couple of years later; the Indian studies program was born, offering two classes; and Sammy the Sioux was shipped off. The "Fighting Sioux" nickname, however, remained as a symbol of the team. With it came all the unfortunate embellishments: portrayals of Indian women having oral sex with buffalo and team chants like "Scalp the Sioux" from opposing teams.

For the next two decades, Native students, members of the American Indian movement, and other groups who opposed the use of the Sioux mascot always met with staunch opposition from the university community, and often from Grand Forks residents and businesses themselves. At one point, several businesses in Grand Forks posted signs in their storefronts that read, "Redskins, go back to the reservations, Leave the name alone."[26]

In l992, Native students created a Seven Feathers Club, a traditional dance club for Native youth, and participated in the homecoming parade at the University of North Dakota. The Seven Feathers Club's float in the parade was followed by one of the UND's Greek community. The fraternity and sorority students taunted the Native children, with phrases like "Go back to the Reservation," "Dirty Indians," and "Tell your parents to get off welfare." When the Native students protested, then UND President Kendall Baker ordered the fraternity and sorority members to apologize and attend multicultural events and created two educational forums a year. The University of North Dakota, however, would not change its name.[27]

The following spring, the University Faculty Senate passed a resolution supporting a name change. The president responded, "It is decided that the name will not be changed because of the great feeling of pride and tradition; the real issue is the need for more education about diverse cultures, using the royalties from the sanctioned logo to fund scholarships for Native American students, cultural programming at athletic events, and assistance for the various UND Native American organizations."[28]

The proposed logo fund, however, was deemed to be "blood money" by the Native students, and every program declined receipt of the money. A resolution to discontinue the use of the Fighting Sioux nickname narrowly passed the student legislature in January of 1999, but then Student Body President Jonathon Sickler vetoed the resolution.[29]

Almost seventy years after the controversy began, the debate deepened as the University of North Dakota began deliberation once again on the name change, largely as the university saw the vast number of colleges nationally who had, rather seamlessly it appeared, changed their names. The university also felt the political pressure from the tribes (ten separate tribal governments had passed resolutions calling for the name change), along with the student body.

The Native students and their supporters had waged a pretty good struggle on the name change, even securing an internal memorandum from President Kupchella, as to what he would say to the board, arguing, "I see no choice but to respect the request of Sioux tribe that we quit using their name, because to do otherwise would be to put the university and its president in an untenable position."[30]

Unfortunately, those words were never spoken; instead, Ralph Englestad's words were heard, loud and clear. Englestad sent a letter to President Kupchella threatening that he would "turn off the building's heat, and take a $35 million loss" if the university changed its name from the Fighting Sioux. Ralph's letter thinly veiled his threats. Less than a week after receipt of the Englestad letter, the university announced there would be no name change.[31]

Ralph Engelstad built his shrine in the North, the most opulent and grandiose shrine to hockey in the world. The immense building does look like the Reichstadt, the huge German amphitheater in which Hitler would amass crowds and then work them into a frenzy of the Third Reich. There are, after all, 11,400 leather seats, armrests cut from cherry wood from Valley Forge, tiles from India, chandeliers from Italy, escalators from Germany, and of course a $2 million scoreboard and even a twenty-four-man Jacuzzi!

Then there is the appropriation itself. The initial gift from Ralph Englestad was to include $50 million for the hockey arena and $50 million for other programs at the university. In the end, Ralph's arena ate up the entire gift. Faculty members, according to a *Sports Illustrated* article (October 8, 2001), "accuse Engelstad of intentionally overspending to punish them for their opposition to the Fighting Sioux nickname and logo. They point to the arenas many extravagances, including a 400-foot hedge that spells out FIGHTNG SIOUX for planes flying overhead . . . 'How much was spent on spite?' 'How much of what he added is him saying, You will get none of my money.'"[32]

In October of 2001, Ralph Engelstad walked to center ice of his own Reichstadt on opening night of the hockey season to a deafening roar of applause. "May this arena keep producing the finest hockey team in the nation. . . . And may the Fighting Sioux and the Fighting Sioux logo stand forever. . . . Our family, and many others did not go." Charlene Teters, a spokesperson for the National Coalition on Racism in Sports and the Media, reiterates the problem, "Using our names, likeness, or religious symbols to excite a crowd does not feel like an honor or respect. It is hurtful and confusing to our young people. To reduce the victims of genocide to a mascot is callous and unthinking at best and immoral at worst."[33]

Although the University of North Dakota has been castigated by *Sports Illustrated* and the *Chronicle of Higher Education*, its neighboring universities, including the University of Minnesota, are very cautious in criticizing the "folds of the family." With increasing private and corporate contributions to the university system, one would hope there is a line to be drawn someplace as to when the price exacted on the integrity of an institution is too high, and the impact on the students within that university too difficult to bear.

There are many more positive ways of honoring Native students and Native People. One hundred million dollars in programs for Native students, tenured faculty, research, and other programs that directly benefit Native communities would be a far more tangible method of honoring Native People. In the meantime, the University of North Dakota and other universities should undertake some soul searching about taking money from various sources, in particular Nazis.

My personal suggestion for an appropriate name for the University of North Dakota's sports teams: The Mighty Sandbaggers. After all, that's what a town built in a floodplain is particularly good at doing.

Notes

1. The Crazy Horse Defense Project web site, www.crazyhorsedefense .org/, accessed October 2002.

2. *News from Indian Country*, Associated Press, March 2002, 4A.

3. Fighting Whites intramural basketball team, www.fightingwhites .org, official home page, accessed October 2002.

4. *News from Indian Country*.

5. D. Nigoya, "Mascot Foes March into Eaton; Fightin' Reds Protest Given Quiet Response," *Denver Post*, May 20, 2002. Accessed December 1, 2002, from www.denverpost.com/framework/0,1918,36%7E53%7E622747%7E,00.html.

6. "In whose honor" refers to the Charlene Teters film that focuses on the subject of mascots and depicts the story of the University of Illinois's Fighting Illini. Produced by Jay Rosenstein. Harriman, NY: New Day Films, 1997.

7. Foster Stangell, "Minnesota Tribes Honored for Excellence in Governing," *The Circle*, December 2000, 8.

8. C. Richard King and Charles Fruehling Springwood, *Team Spirits: The Native American Mascots Controversy* (Lincoln: University of Nebraska Press, 2001).

9. Dr. Cornel Pewewardy, "Insult or Honor? Indian Mascots in School Related Events," guest commentary in *News from Indian Country*, September 2000, 17A.

10. Helena Norberg Hodge, "Shifting Direction, from Global Dependence to Local Interdependence," in *Case Against the Global Economy*, edited by Jerry Mander and Edward Goldsmith (San Francisco: Sierra Club Books, 1996), 393–395. Hodge writes about Ladakah in the Himalayas.

11. King and Springwood, *Team Spirits*.

12. Carol Spindel, *Dancing at Halftime: Sports and the Controversy over American Indian Mascots* (New York: New York University Press, 2000), 29.

13. King and Springwood, *Team Spirits*, 10.

14. Roland Barthes, *Mythologies* (New York: Hill and Wang, 1972).

15. Spindel, *Dancing at Halftime*, 28.

16. Teters, quoted in Spindel, *Dancing at Halftime*, 32–33.

17. Andrew Bronstein, "A Battle Over a Name in the Land of the Sioux," *The Chronicle of Higher Education*, February 23, 2001.

18. Bronstein, "A Battle Over a Name."

19. Bronstein, "A Battle Over a Name."

20. Ralph K. Andrist, *The Long Death: The Last Days of the Plains Indians* (New York: Collier-Macmillan, 1969), 343–344.

21. Bob Gough, interview from *Native America Calling*, September 3, 2002.

22. Gough, interview from *Native America Calling*.

23. Bronstein, "A Battle Over a Name."

24. Holly Annis "Fighting the 'Fighting Sioux' Tradition," *Native Directions* 6, no. 2 (1999), from Native Media Center, the School of Communications, UND.

25. Annis, "Fighting the 'Fighting Sioux' Tradition."

26. Annis, "Fighting the 'Fighting Sioux' Tradition."

27. Annis, "Fighting the 'Fighting Sioux' Tradition."

28. *Native Directions*, 1999.

29. Annis, "Fighting the 'Fighting Sioux' Tradition," 3.

30. *Native Directions*, 1999.

31. Howie Padilla, "Old Issue Comes with New Area: Fighting Sioux Still Riles," *Minneapolis Star Tribune*, October 6, 2001.

32. "North Dakota Opens Hockey Arena Amid Nickname Flap," *Sports Illustrated*, October 2001.

33. Padilla, "Old Issue Comes with New Area."

II

CONTESTATION
AND POLITICS

6

Native American Resistance and Revitalization in the Era of Self-Determination

Troy R. Johnson

Many of the federal government's legislative changes and much of the contemporary awareness of Native American issues have their roots firmly planted in the post–World War II era. Identified by names such as the American Indian Youth Council, United Native Americans, Indians of All Tribes, Women of All Red Nations, and the American Indian Movement, American Indian activist groups made up primarily of young Native Americans protested against treaty violations, termination, urban relocation, reservation unemployment, violence, and other forms of discrimination against American Indian people, including attempts at detribalization and assaults on the remaining Indian land base. These acts of protest demanded recognition of treaty rights, protection of fishing and hunting rights, and protection of religious freedoms, and put forth a new demand for recognition of Indian self-determination and tribal sovereignty.

American Indian activists learned from and built upon the larger social conditions present in America at that time. The 1960s and early 1970s were heady times for urban unrest across the United States. The civil rights movement, Black Power, the rise of LaRaza, the stirring of the new feminism, the rise of the New Left Generation, and the Third World Strikes were sweeping the nation, particularly college campuses. People of all ages were becoming sensitized to the unrest among the emerging minority ethnic and gender groups, particularly among the vocal and active college student populations. Sit-ins, sleep-ins, teach-ins, lock-outs, and boycotts became everyday occurrences on college campuses. Young Native Americans who had come to the urban areas through the relocation program were now enrolled in colleges and universities where they watched and learned from the experiences of the other emerging ethnic power groups. The roots of their unrest were stretching toward the future; however, they were firmly planted and nourished in the past.

During and following World War II, the federal government, responding to a national conservative movement, passed a series of laws implementing the termination of Indian reservations. The explicit intent was the unilateral termination of the U.S. relationship with Indian tribes. Between 1954 and 1962 more than one hundred bands, communities, tribes, and Indian rancherias were severed from direct relations with the federal government. Indian Nations and Native American people lost many protections and services that had been guaranteed by the U.S. government in the eighteenth and nineteenth centuries in exchange for the surrender of millions of acres of valuable land and confinement on small, often uninhabitable, parcels of land.

Termination was a complete reversal of the previous government policy of Indian Reorganization and was designed to officially end tribal self-government, health care, cultural and tribal bonds, and most federal obligations to Indian people that had been contained in past treaties, executive orders, or acts of Congress. Tribal self-government was now seen as impeding the assimilation of Indian people into the dominant society as full, taxpaying citizens. Dillon Myer, the former director of the War Relocation Authority (WRA), became commissioner of Indian affairs in 1950 and was a strong advocate of termination of Indian reservations and forced assimilation. He displayed his total ignorance of Indian history, culture, and contribution to American society when he spoke before the National Congress of American Indians in 1950 and stated that Indians [the first Americans] "had a responsibility as American citizens to become a productive society" (Senese 1991). Myer was also a strong supporter of the relocation of reservation Indian people to urban centers. He had relocated thousands of loyal Japanese Americans from urban cities to relocation camps; now he felt it his duty to relocate thousands of Indian people from reservations to urban cities.

House Concurrent Resolution 108 (HCR 108) was adopted in 1953 and attacked Native American tribal landholding and political existence and created a climate of fear throughout Indian Country. The act expressed Congress's growing unrest regarding its special relationship with Indian tribes and moved for termination of this federal relationship as rapidly as possible. The act stated:

> That it is declared to be the sense of Congress that, *at the earliest possible time*, all of the Indian tribes within the States of California, Florida, New York, and Texas . . . should be freed from Federal supervision and control and from all disabilities and limitations specially applicable to Indians [to detribalize Indian people and separate them from their traditional homelands]. (Getches et al. 1998)

The Senate heard HCR 108 on August 2, 1953, and endorsed the resolution without debate. While it is true that HCR 108 passed without debate, that is not to say that Native American people did not recognize the intent of the resolution. Tribal delegates expressed their concerns regarding the pending legislation and participated in nine of the thirteen hearings held. Some appeared as tribal delegates, and some spoke on their own behalf. Some Indian Nations were able to pay the way for delegates to attend the hearings and sent large groups. The poorest tribes were either unrepresented or had only a single member present. A small number of tribes and individuals favored removal from government control and the liquidation of reservations in order to receive their personal share of tribal property. They expressed a desire to be able to remove their tribal property from federal trust states and to sell or mortgage their property as they so chose. Many of these individuals were urban Indian people with only limited contact with the reservation communities who felt little connectedness with the tribal group.

HCR 108 was a statement of policy, however, and individual acts of Congress were necessary to implement the policy regarding specific tribes. The fear being experienced by Native American people intensified when it became obvious that Indian Nations would have no voice in the matter of termination and that Congress intended to apply extreme pressure on tribes to accept full termination of the federal trust relationship. Lacking clear judicial authority to end the federal relationship with Indian Nations, the authority to terminate tribal sovereignty was found in the doctrine of "plenary power." The plenary power doctrine is a principle that reflects the awesome power of Congress to "repeal, abrogate, or amend Indian treaties even though they [treaties] are the supreme law of the land" (Getches et al. 1998). The exercise of the plenary power doctrine can best be seen in the court case *Lone Wolf v. Hitchcock*. In this 1903 court case, the U.S. Supreme Court stated that "plenary authority over the tribal relations of the Indians has been exercised by Congress from the beginning and the power has always been deemed a political one, not subject to be controlled by the judicial department of the government" (Getches et al. 1998).

Termination had a devastating effect on the terminated Nations and their people. Tribal land ownership was altered drastically. Land could now be sold to third parties, transferred to private trusts, or transferred to new corporations developed under state law. All special programs for the terminated Native Nations were discontinued, as were special federal programs such as health and education to individual Indian people. State legislative and judicial jurisdiction was imposed except in areas of hunting and fishing rights, exemptions for state taxing was ended, and, more destructively, tribal sovereignty as recognized in the watershed 1832 court case *Worcester v. Georgia* was severely challenged (Getches et al. 1998).

A critical component of the federal program to terminate Indian tribes and to encourage assimilation was the relocation of Indian people into urban areas. Between 1950 and 1965 some 200,000 Native People accepted the promises offered by the relocation program. They saw relocation as an opportunity to improve their lives. Survival on the remaining Indian reservations in the 1950s was difficult. Most reservations were without electricity or running water. Health and life expectancy were the lowest for any group in America. Suicide and accidental deaths were the highest in the nation. For tens of thousands of Indian people, however, the relocation program involved little more than exchanging reservation poverty for urban poverty. Relocatees were to be provided housing, training, and job referrals to put them on the road to self-reliance. Promised housing proved to be 1950s skid-row apartments. Job training was limited to few choices. Men could become welders or plumbers, and women were trained as typists or domestics. Although many Indian people were discouraged or disillusioned and returned to the reservations, large numbers of Indian people remained in the urban cities and formed a substantial urban Indian population. In cities such as Oakland, Denver, Minneapolis, Los Angeles, and Chicago, these urban Indians banded together in small social groups that over time evolved into Indian centers such as the San Francisco Indian Center. The larger centers took on an urban "pan-Indian" persona and became politically active, as well as providing for the social and cultural needs of the people. It would be out of these urban Indian centers and communities that the Native American activism and Red Power movement of the late 1950s, 1960s, and early 1970s would grow (Johnson 1996, 1997).

Stephen Cornell and Joane Nagel (Cornell 1988; Nagel 1996) provide the most current and persuasive discussions regarding the rise of a pan-Indian movement and the contribution these groups made to Native American activism, particularly in the 1960s and early 1970s. They argue that the past policies of the federal government, such as allotment, termination, and relocation, fueled a nascent movement that came into full bloom in the form of a Red Power movement. By 1960, young Indian people, particularly in the urban areas, began to question the wisdom of Native elders who had attempted to pursue Indian justice through "the white man's court." The wheels of justice, for these young Native People, turned excruciatingly slow, and often it was Native treaty rights and individual rights that were crushed beneath the wheel. In 1961, an activist organization, the National Indian Youth Council (NIYC), was created as a spin-off of the more tradition-bound National Congress of American Indians (NCAI). Clyde Warrior, a Ponca Indian, and Melvin Thom, a Paiute, were two of the founding members. The NIYC challenged the approaches of traditional advocacy groups such as the NCAI and the Indian Rights Association. The council represented a younger Indian voice and presented an activist orientation to solving Indian problems.

Vine Deloria, Jr., Standing Rock Sioux writer, lawyer, and professor emeritus from the University of Colorado, Boulder, is generally recognized as the leading scholar on American Indian history, culture, and religion in the nation. His book *Custer Died for Your Sins*, published in 1969, opened the eyes of Americans, Indian and non-Indian, to the condition and treatment of Native Peoples at that time. Writing at a time when American Indian people had largely been forgotten, Deloria encouraged scholars to examine Indian history through the use of irony and satire, to gain a better understanding of the collective psyche and values of Native American people.

Since 1969, Deloria has published an impressive number of books that further explore and validate the complicity of the federal government in the near genocide of Native Nations and Native People. His 1985 book, *American Indian Policy in the Twentieth Century*, provides the reader with a valuable introduction to the changing policies that have adversely affected Native Americans (Deloria 1985). In his most recent book, *Tribes, Treaties, and Constitutional Tribulations*, which he coauthored with David E. Wilkins and published in 2000, Deloria delivers an indictment of constitutional law as it applies to American Indian people. In this book Deloria traces the roots of Indian sovereignty to the founding of America and the U.S. Constitution. This is especially important in understanding where Indian people are today in the political arena and why Indian people have been successful in overcoming individual state challenges to their sovereignty in issues of water rights, land use, and gaming on Indian reservations.

It is impossible to affix an exact beginning date for the rise of the Red Power movement; however, few would disagree that the fishing rights struggle that began in 1963 in the state of Washington was a significant factor. In December 1963 a state of Washington court ruled against Indian fishing rights that had been guaranteed to the Indian tribes in various treaties with the federal government that allowed Indian people to fish in "all usual and accustomed places," including off-reservation traditional fishing locations. This was a serious attack on guaranteed treaty rights and sovereignty for the Nations concerned. Non-Indian sports fishermen and commercial fishermen supported the court decision and began to harass and intimidate Indian fishermen who dared to venture into their legal fishing grounds in an attempt to survive. Resistance by Indians ran strong, however, and in 1964, an American Indian of Lakota and Assiniboine ancestry, Hank Adams, coordinated the efforts of the NIYC, and a group of Indian activists assisted by the Survival of American Indians Association (SAIA), to bring the demands of

Indian fishermen to the Washington state capitol in Olympia. By mid-1964 a new term, "fish-ins" had been born. The fish-ins represented a creative civil rights tactic that had its roots and was perhaps borrowed from the lunch counter desegregation "sit-ins" of the nascent Black Power movement of the early 1960s. Hank focused his attention on the Nisqually River near Franks Landing, Washington, where he protested state attempts to limit Indian net fishing. In January 1971, Adams was shot in the stomach, on the banks of the Puyallup River near Tacoma, Washington, where he was tending a fishing trap. He survived the wound, however, and continued his fight for enforcement of Indian fishing rights (Johnson 1996).

The unrest and frustration that motivated Hank Adams and led to the fish-ins were not unique to the Pacific Northwest. Indian people across the United States felt betrayed by a government that had taken their lands and given broken treaty promises in return. Urban Indian people were among the most forgotten. Many, or most, had been dumped in urban areas during the relocation era without adequate housing, training, support, finances, or direction. By 1968, one group of Indian people in Minneapolis, Minnesota, had had enough. On July 28, 1968, an organization, The American Indian Movement (AIM), was founded by a group of urban Indians protesting police brutality. Minneapolis police, who were overwhelmingly white, waited outside of "Indian bars" at closing time and beat, abused, and arrested Indian men and women. In Minneapolis, where only 10 percent of the population was Indian, 70 percent of the city jail inmates were Indians. From 1968 to November 1970 AIM concentrated its efforts in the Minneapolis and St. Paul, Minnesota, cities. AIM leaders began to make appearances at national Indian conferences as well, where they set up tables and passed out AIM materials. AIM would ultimately become the most sophisticated and nationally recognized Indian activist group, with branches throughout the United States, but they needed a national audience and a springboard to catapult them onto the national scene.

Native Americans heard, observed, and studied the civil rights movement that was sweeping the country. Urban American Indian people, under the leadership of Jack Forbes (Powhatan/Lenape), Richard Oakes (Mohawk), and LaNada Boyer (Shoshoni/Bannock), formed such groups as United Native Americans (UNA) and Indians of All Tribes (IOAT) to aggressively pursue Indian rights. On the Berkeley campus of the University of California, Native American scholar Jack Forbes and his Indian students located an unused bungalow, occupied it, and later received permission to develop a native cultural center (Johnson 1996, 1997).

In March 1966, President Lyndon Johnson attempted to quiet the fears of Indian people. In a speech before the Senate, he proposed a "new goal that erases old attitudes of paternalism and promotes partnerships in self-help"(*Public Papers of the Presidents of the United States: Lyndon B. Johnson, 1968–69*, vol. I, 336–337). On April 11, 1969, the National Council on Indian Opportunity (NCIO), established by President Johnson, conducted a public forum before the Committee on Urban Indians in San Francisco. The purpose was to gain as much information as possible on the condition of the Native Americans living in the San Francisco area and to find solutions to their problems and ease the rising tensions. Earl Livermore (Goshute/Blackfoot), director of the San Francisco American Indian Center, appeared before the committee and testified about problems Indian people faced in adjusting to urban living, particularly Indian students faced with unfavorable conditions in the public school system. Those conditions included false and misleading statements in school textbooks that damaged the Indian child's sense of identity and personal worth. His testimony included urban Indian health problems that led to frustration and depression. Lack of education resulted in unemployment, unemployment led to depression, and depression led Native Americans deeper into the depths of despair. Richard Oakes (Mohawk) reiterated Livermore's call for college courses relevant to American Indians and called for new textbooks that accurately portrayed the role of American Indians in U.S. history.

A reporter asked LaDonna Harris, a Comanche Indian and chair of the committee, "Are you going to have some militant Indians?" Harris replied, "Heavens, I hope we will." LaDonna's appeal was answered on November 20, 1969, when Indian students occupied Alcatraz Island, claiming title by "right of discovery." Once on the island, the occupiers formed an Alcatraz organization, Indians of All Tribes (IOAT), and issued a proclamation to the U.S. government and to the American people demanding that the federal government grant them title to Alcatraz Island, build an Indian university, an American Indian cultural center, and an American Indian museum. IOAT sent speakers across the United States to inform other Native Nations of the importance of the occupation. They published a newsletter, *Rock Talk*, and broadcast twice weekly over "Radio Free Alcatraz" (Johnson 1996).

The mood of the public was in support of the occupiers. President Richard Nixon received thousands of letters and telegrams urging him to transfer title of Alcatraz Island to IOAT. One telegram summed up the public feeling: "For once in this country's history let the Indians have something. Let them have Alcatraz." On July 8, 1970, President Nixon announced a new Indian policy of Indian self-determination without termination, and on December 15, President Nixon returned Taos Blue Lake and 48,000 acres of land to the Taos Pueblo people. Leonard Garment, Nixon's Indian adviser, related the return of Blue Lake directly to the occupiers on Alcatraz. Garment stated, "A new Indian policy needs a starting point. Blue Lake is just that—strong on merits, and powerfully symbolic. . . . The return of Taos Blue Lake is a nationwide symbol of this Administration's new approach toward Indian affairs" (Gordon-McCutchan 1991).

In *The Taos Indians and the Battle for Blue Lake*, Gordon-McCutchan provides perhaps the best insight ever into the relationship between the White House and Indian issues. Gordon-McCutchan traces not only the history of the taking of Taos Blue Lake from the Taos people but the interworkings of the White House to insure that President Nixon's declared policy of Indian self-determination was truly reflected in dealings with Native Peoples. The Indian occupiers successfully held the island until June 11, 1971, at which time they were removed by officials of the General Services Administration, FBI, and U.S. Marshals Service. By that time, however, Alcatraz had become a rallying cry for the new American Indian activism sweeping the nation under the name of Red Power and The American Indian Movement. It has been estimated that during the nineteen-month occupation, over 15,000 American Indian people visited the island.

Some of them stayed for days or weeks, and some for the entire nineteen-month period. New leaders emerged: Richard Oakes (Mohawk), LaNada Boyer (Shoshoni/Bannock), and John Trudell (Santee Sioux). Occupiers left the island and went on to lead the occupation of other facilities, many of which were former military bases, CIA listening posts, and national monuments. Following the Alcatraz occupation there were occupations of over sixty other facilities. The leaders of those occupations stated that they had been on Alcatraz Island or were inspired by the Alcatraz occupation.

Members of AIM visited Alcatraz Island during the summer of 1970. They made recommendations regarding island security and saw firsthand that the federal government's hands were tied because of public support and news media coverage. This was best demonstrated by a statement made by President Nixon: "The American public will not stand by and see American Indians taken off of Alcatraz Island in body bags" (Johnson 1996). The springboard for AIM's rise to national prominence was now in place.

Following AIM's visit to Alcatraz Island, AIM leaders Dennis Banks (Anishinabe), Russell Means (Oglala-Yankton Sioux), and Clyde Bellecourt (Ojibwa) began to plot the course for the organization. On Thanksgiving Day, 1970, they made their first move and seized control of the *Mayflower II* in Plymouth, Massachusetts. Means and members of twenty-five Indian tribes proclaimed Thanksgiving a national day of mourning to protest the taking of Native American lands. Means acknowledged the occupation of Alcatraz Island as the symbol of a newly awakened desire of the Indians for unity and authority in a white world. They next buried Plymouth Rock under several inches of sand.

By 1971 AIM had made the Twin Cities of Minnesota their operational headquarters. In May 1971 AIM members occupied an abandoned naval air station near Minneapolis and cited the Sioux Treaty of 1868 as their authority, just as the Indian occupiers of Alcatraz Island had in 1969. The occupiers were removed from the air station five days later but not before they had formed a governing structure and security system similar to those on Alcatraz and issued a petition to the federal government similar to that of Indians of All Tribes.

Following the naval air station occupation at Minneapolis in May 1971 and continuing through October 1972, there were thirteen major occupations led by AIM and IOAT, including Nike missile bases, an abandoned Coast Guard lifeboat station, and the Twin Cities Naval Air Station. Attempted occupations of the Statue of Liberty and the Washington, D.C., office of the Bureau of Indian Affairs (BIA) ended in arrests and confiscation of property. In the summer of 1971, members of IOAT and AIM traveled to Wounded Knee, South Dakota, for a Sun Dance being performed by Wallace

Black Elk, John Lame Deer, and Leonard Crow Dog. This was the unification of former members of IOAT with AIM, now recognized as a national Indian activist organization (Johnson 1996). The Alcatraz occupation was the catalyst for the rise of the 1972 occupation of the Washington, D.C., BIA headquarters occupation, the 1973 occupation of Wounded Knee, and the rise of the American Indian Movement (AIM) to national prominence as a nationally recognized Indian activist group.

The history of the American Indian Movement and their "war" with the Federal Bureau of Investigation is best portrayed in Peter Matthiessen's book *In the Spirit of Crazy Horse: The Story of Leonard Peltier and the FBI's War on the American Indian Movement*. The history of the publication of *In the Spirit of Crazy Horse* rivals that of the story it tells. In 1983, Viking Press stopped the presses after former South Dakota governor William Janklow and FBI special agent David Price launched lawsuits against Matthiessen seeking a total of $55 million in damages, claiming that Matthiessen had libeled them, portraying them as "morally decadent" and "corrupt and vicious" individuals. Ultimately a South Dakota judge dismissed the lawsuits, finding Matthiessen's account to be "fair and balanced" and declaring that Matthiessen had a constitutional right to state his opinion. The judge praised the publisher (Viking Press) for its determination to undertake the publication of such "difficult but important works." With the favorable ruling, *In the Spirit of Crazy Horse* was published in 1992 by Penguin Books and is still considered by many people to be the seminal work on the American Indian Movement.

Between October and November 1972, more than five hundred Indian protesters participated in the "Trail of Broken Treaties." The idea for the march began on the Sioux Reservation in 1972 as an attempt to sensitize the Republican and Democratic parties to the problems faced by Native Americans. Although many people supported the idea of such a march, a catalyst was needed to spur its planning. That came on September 21, 1972, when Richard Oakes, one of the Alcatraz occupation leaders, was shot to death by a YMCA guard in northern California. AIM leaders including Russell Means and Hank Adams held a press conference in Seattle to denounce the murder. One week later fifty Indian people gathered at the New Albany Hotel in Denver to formalize plans for a march on Washington, D.C. Some would come from the West Coast; the Sioux passed by Wounded Knee, the sight of the 1890 massacre. When the caravan arrived in Washington and found that the accommodations promised them were not available, the group moved to the BIA headquarters building. The occupiers demanded that they be allowed to meet with President Nixon; however, leaders of the caravan were aware that Nixon was not in Washington, D.C., at that time.

On November 2, in a disagreement over housing and food provisions, members of the Trail of Broken Treaties occupied and barricaded the BIA building and presented a list of twenty civil rights demands that had been drawn up during the march. These included a repeal of the 1871 ban on Indian treaties, restoration of treaty-making status to individual tribes, provision of full government services to unrecognized eastern tribes, review of all past treaty violations, restitution for those violations, demands that Public Law 180 be repealed, that tribes be given criminal jurisdiction over non-Indians on reservations, and that cultural and economic conditions for Indians be improved. Native Americans occupied the BIA building for seven days. Inside the building the Indians, fearing retaliation for the BIA headquarters, began a wave of violence against the building and against the policies for which it stood. Looting and trashing were widespread, as was the destruction of documents, artwork, and records of government policies affecting Indian people. Eventually the government promised to review the demands, refrain from making arrests, and pay the Indians' expenses home. The occupation came to an end on November 8, 1972.

The occupation was a great moral victory for AIM and the NIYC who directed the march. Other sponsoring groups included the National Indian Brotherhood of Canada, the Survival of American Indians Association, the National American Indian Council, the Native American Rights Fund, the National Council on Indian Work, the American Indian Commission of Aicchol and Drug Abuse, and the National Indian Leadership Training. Indian people and Indian organizations had come together as never before in an effort to confront the U.S. government.

AIM leaders and members felt like they had scored a major victory during the BIA headquarters occupation despite the destruction of government property. This occupation plus the thirteen that preceded it made AIM a household word among Indian people. Indian tribes and Indian people in trouble felt they now had an organization they could call upon for help in time of distress. AIM members enjoyed their new status as modern-day Indian warriors. They did not have to wait long to be tested in battle.

On January 21, 1973, Darrell Schmitz, a thirty-year-old white man, stabbed a Sioux man, Wesley Bad Heart Bull, to death on the streets of Buffalo Gap, South Dakota. Schmitz was charged with second-degree manslaughter, the weakest charge possible, even though there were four witnesses to the stabbing. AIM members insisted that the charge should have been one of murder. On February 6, 1973, approximately two hundred American Indian people, many belonging to AIM, arrived in Custer, South Dakota, to protest Bad Heart Bull's murder. Russell Means and four other AIM members led the protest. Fighting broke out on the Custer Courthouse steps when AIM was refused entrance into the courtroom. Sarah Bad Heart Bull, mother of Wesley, was grabbed, choked, beaten, and arrested by police when she attempted to identify the four witnesses to her son's slaying. Native Americans who tried to come to her assistance were attacked with clubs, tear gas, mace, and water hoses and were also arrested. Several hundred members of the National Guard were called to active duty to restore peace in the area. Thirty Indian people were arrested and sixty-five U.S. marshals were assigned to Pine Ridge to enforce security and to conduct surveillance of AIM (Smith and Warrior 1996).

By late 1972 AIM members seemed to be everywhere. This is an overstatement of fact; however, their presence was especially strong in the Great Plains states, such as North and South Dakota. These two states were known for their racist attitudes, brutality, and discrimination against Native people. Wesley Bad Heart Bull was only one of a growing number of Indian people who were killed, and no one was being punished. This is not to say, however, that everyone supported AIM. Some tribal leaders saw AIM as a threat to their leadership. On the Pine Ridge Indian Reservation, the BIA elected chairman, Richard (Dickey) Wilson, nurtured a virulent hatred for AIM and its leaders. He denounced the AIM takeover of the BIA headquarters in Washington, D.C., and AIM's involvement in the Custer City melee. He also saw AIM, particularly Russell Means, as a threat to his position as tribal chairman. In 1971 an AIM chapter was formed on the Pine Ridge Reservation, further exacerbating the situation. In 1972 Wilson warned AIM to stay away from the Pine Ridge Reservation, going so far as to threaten to cut off Russell Mean's braids if he dared to enter Pine Ridge (Smith and Warrior 1996).

Life on the Pine Ridge Reservation was difficult. Pine Ridge led the nation in poverty, alcoholism, infant death, suicide, and poor health care. In the early 1970s unemployment, except for members of Chairman Wilson's circle of kinspeople, ran as high as 90 percent and averaged over 85 percent. On February 27, 1973, a group of two hundred Native Americans, led by AIM and supported by Alcatraz occupiers, congregated at the site of the 1890 Wounded Knee Massacre to demonstrate against Wilson, whom they charged with corrupt practices. The Sioux traditionalists, who did not accept the IRA government as represented by Wilson, had actually called AIM for help when Wilson and his Government of the Oglala Nation (GOON) squads began beatings and shootings to enforce Wilson's rule. Tensions between the protesters and the local authorities grew until the situation became a siege of the town that drew in two hundred Indians from around the area and lasted for seventy-one days. The occupiers were surrounded by three hundred federal marshals and FBI agents equipped with Vietnam-era armored personnel carriers, M16s, automatic infantry weapons, chemical weapons, steel helmets, gas masks, body armor, illuminating flares, military clothing, and almost unlimited rations. The army's 82nd Airborne Division provided leadership and logistical support for the government "peacekeeping" force.

On March 12 the occupiers declared Wounded Knee a sovereign territory of the new Oglala Sioux Nation according to the Laramie Treaty of 1868, which recognized the Sioux as an independent nation. The Wounded Knee occupation finally ended on the morning of May 8, 1973, when the two sides began firing on each other and two Indians, Frank Clearwater and Lawrence (Buddy) Lamont, were shot and killed, an act that called national attention to the Native American civil rights movement. One federal marshal was shot and permanently paralyzed. Two hundred and thirty-seven arrests were made, and thirty-five weapons were confiscated. Russell Means and Dennis Banks were arraigned on ten felony counts in a trial that lasted eight months. In February 1974, in a hotly contested and rigged election, Dickey Wilson barely defeated Means as tribal chairman. Wilson's supporters ordered all those who voted for Means off of the reservation and terrorized AIM members and their families.

Means was shot in the kidney by a BIA officer and arraigned for assault. AIM leaders spent the majority of their time after the Wounded Knee occupation preparing for court, in court, or in jail. The AIM organization had difficulty maintaining national coherency. Indian issues were different in different parts of the country, and local AIM chapters with local leaders emerged. The FBI continued its now relentless, dogmatic program of destruction of the organization. Phones were tapped, surveillance increased, moles (spies) were placed within the organization, and suspected AIM members simply disappeared. Many feel to this day that the FBI assassinated over 150 AIM members (Matthiessen 1992). The papers of Senator James G. Abourezk contain a wealth of material relating to the federal government's attitude and reaction to the Wounded Knee occupation. Abourezk volunteered to act as a peace negotiator between the government and the Indians; however, he was unable to resolve the differences between the Indian occupiers of Wounded Knee and Dickey Wilson and the Oglala tribal IRA government (Abourezk 1973).

There can be little doubt that the activism of the 1960s and 1970s, while unpopular among some Indian people, and in some cases unsuccessful in reaching its immediate goals, had a profound and positive impact on government policy toward the Indian Nations. The oft-spoken goal of the activists was one of self-determination for Indian people—the rights of Indians to handle their own affairs with as little government intervention as possible. Clyde Warrior, a Ponca Indian and cofounder of the National Indian Youth Council (NIYC), explained the powerlessness and lack of self-determination to government officials in Washington in 1967. The rhetoric of Indian self-determination can be traced to the early '60s, when Melvin Thom, a Paiute Indian from Walker River, Nevada, and a cofounder and president of NIYC, recognized the need to alleviate the poverty, unemployment, and degrading lifestyles forced on both urban and reservation Indians. Thom realized that it was essential that Indian people, Indian tribes, and Indian sovereign rights not be compromised in the search for solutions to their many problems.

In a sense, Indian self-determination was an offshoot of the government policy of termination of Indian tribes and tribal people.

By the mid-1960s the government recognized that the termination policy was a failure. Termination was destroying Indian Nations and creating a financial burden on the federal and state governments as Indian people were pushed onto welfare roles and public assistance. In an effort to ameliorate the situation, the new Democratic administration of President Lyndon Johnson introduced government programs under the auspices of the Office of Economic Opportunity aimed at eliminating poverty on Indian reservations. President Richard Nixon followed the lead of President Johnson and personally introduced legislation to improve the life of Indian people.

On July 8, 1970, President Richard Nixon began his address to Congress by repudiating the government policy of termination of Indian tribes. President Nixon acknowledged the unconscionable plight of American Indians when he stated, "The first Americans— the Indians are the most deprived and most isolated minority group in our nation. On virtually every scale of measurement—employment, income, education, health—the conditions of the Indian people rank at the bottom." Nixon announced a new policy of self-determination without termination and stated, "It is long past time that the Indian policies of the Federal government began to recognize and build upon the capacities and insights of the Indian people" (Johnson 1996). Nixon also announced the return of Taos Blue Lake to the Taos Indians as his first step on his pledge of good faith on self-determination. In a memorandum from Leonard Garment, special assistant to Nixon, to Bradley Patterson, Garment stated that he hoped that the meaning of the return of Taos Blue Lake to the Taos people would not be lost to the Indian people still holding Alcatraz Island and calling for Indian self-determination (Gordon-McCutchan 1991).

Perhaps the most exciting legislation affecting Indian people, and certainly in keeping with the twin goals of tribal sovereignty and self-determination, was the passage of the Tribal Self-Governance Act into law. On July 2–3, 1990, Assistant Secretary of the Interior Eddie Brown signed historic agreements with six tribes: Quinault Indian Nation, Tahola, Washington; Lummi Indian Nation, Bellingham, Washington; Jamestown Klallam Indian tribe, Sequim, Washington; Hoopa Valley Indian tribe, Hoopa, California; Cherokee Nation, Tahlequah, Oklahoma; and Mille Lacs band of Chippewa Indians, Onamia, Minnesota. These tribes were part of a self-governance pilot program that would ultimately allow up to twenty tribes the authority to administer and set priorities for federal funds received directly from the government and bypass the control of the BIA. On December 4, 1991, Congress passed legislation to amend the Indian Self-Determination and Education Assistance Act. Entitled the Tribal Self-Governance Demonstration Project, the act extended the number of tribes taking part in the tribal self-governance pilot project from twenty to thirty.

The principles guiding the original negotiation of these compacts, originally defined by Indian leaders in 1986 and 1987, emphasized the establishment of a government-to-government relationship with the United States on a tribe-by-tribe basis. Emphasis was placed on the importance of these agreements being negotiated between each Indian government and the United States government as a whole instead of Indian governments dealing with individual governmental agencies. Thirty-three Native Nations concluded one or more Compacts of Self-Governance with the United States between 1990 and 1995. Three studies were conducted in 1993, 1994, and 1995 to provide annual self-governance assessments. The first study in 1993 emphasized Indian government compliance with compacts and the effectiveness of accounting and budgetary systems. The second and third studies conducted in 1994 and 1995 focused on "costs and benefits," in order to ascertain compliance by Indian governments and officials of the BIA and the Office of Self-Governance.

The annual studies generally approved the creative and effective activities of Indian governments but were critical of the U.S. government's compliance with congressional and compact terms and requirements. The Center for World Indigenous Studies released the Final Report of the Self-Governance Process Evaluation on July 1, 1996. The report states "based on a review of documents (historical and contemporary) that the United States government generally is not seriously participating in the development and conduct of the self-government initiative." The report was encouraging for Native Nations, however, and stated that "Baseline Measures Reports from subject Indian governments and the study conducted by the Department of the Interior (August, 1995) confirms that Indian governments have made major progress toward social and economic development as a direct result of the self-governance initiative" (Ryser 1995).

Many Indian Nations continue to look at self-governance as the best opportunity to exercise national self-determination and to exert tribal sovereignty. In fiscal year 2002, the number of Indian tribes/consortia participating in the Tribal Self-Governance Program increased to eighty, representing some 225 federally recognized Indian Tribes. Additionally, the U.S. government has responded to concerns addressed in the Center for World Indigenous Studies Self-Government Evaluation. Funding for the self-governance initiative increased to $180,407,000 in fiscal year 2002, $181,619,000 in fiscal year 2003, and was estimated to be $184,048,000 in fiscal year 2004 (CFDA 15.022, Office of Management and Budget).

Members of the American Indian Youth Council, United Native Americans, Indians of All Tribes, Women of All Red Nations, and the American Indian Movement can be justly proud of the legacy they have left and the changes that have been made as a result of Indian activism over the past four decades. Indian Nations, and by extension Indian people, participating in self-governance now have the opportunity to exercise discretion in establishing funding priorities for reservation infrastructure and to exercise self-determination in the design of tribal programs, services, and activities in response to local needs and circumstances. While these were not the exact goals as espoused by those young Indian activists, self-governance and sovereignty were indeed the underlying battle cry.

References

Abourezk, James G. Papers 1970–1983, Wounded Knee, 1973 Series Catalogue of Federal Domestic Assistance, 15.022 Tribal Self-Governance.

Champagne, Duane, ed. *The Native North American Almanac: A Reference Work on Native North Americans in the United States and Canada*. Detroit: Gale Research, 1994.

Cornell, Stephen. *The Return of the Native: American Indian Political Resurgence*. New York: Oxford University Press, 1988.

Deloria, Vine, Jr. *American Indian Policy in the Twentieth Century*. Norman: University of Oklahoma Press, 1985.

Getches, David H., Charles F. Wilkinson, and Robert A. Williams, Jr. *Cases and Materials on Federal Indian Law*. Fourth ed. St. Paul, MN: American Casebook Series, West Group, 1998.

Gordon-McCutchan, R. C. *The Taos Indians and the Battle for Blue Lake*. Santa Fe, NM: Red Crane Books, 1991.

Grossman, Mark. *The ABC-CLIO Companion to the Native American Rights Movement*. Santa Barbara, CA: ABC-CLIO, 1996.

Johnson, Troy. *The Occupation of Alcatraz Island: Indian Self-Determination and the Rise of Indian Activism*. Urbana: University of Illinois Press, 1996.

Johnson, Troy, Joane Nagel, and Duane Champagne. *American Indian Activism: Alcatraz to The Longest Walk*. Urbana: University of Illinois Press, 1997.

Matthiessen, Peter. *In the Spirit of Crazy Horse*. New York: Penguin Books, 1992.

Nagel, Joane. *American Indian Ethnic Renewal: Red Power and the Resurgence of Identity and Culture*. New York: Oxford University Press, 1996.

Office of Management and Budget, CFDA (Catalog of Federal Domestic Assistance) 15.022. http://clinton4.nara.gov/OMB/circulars/a133 _compliance/DOI.html., accessed October 2003.

Ryser, Rudolph C., principal investigator. *Indian Self-Government Process Evaluation Project, Preliminary Findings*. Olympia, WA: Center for World Indigenous Studies, 1995.

Senese, Guy B. *Self-Determination and the Social Education of Native Americans*. New York: Praeger, 1991.

Smith, Paul C., and Robert Allen Warrior. *Like A Hurricane: The Indian Movement from Alcatraz to Wounded Knee*. New York: The New Press, 1996.

7

Oral Tradition, Identity, and Intergenerational Healing through the Southern Paiute Salt Songs

Melissa K. Nelson

Every year for the past five years I have had the great opportunity to travel to the Southern Paiute territory of the American Southwest and work with Paiute elders and leaders on their own community-initiated projects. I do this work as an individual researcher and writer through the American Indian Studies Department at San Francisco State University and as an indigenous rights activist through the Cultural Conservancy. A lot of this work is done with my friend and colleague Philip M. Klasky through the Cultural Conservancy. In this work I strive to embody a creative convergence of indigenous scholarship and community activism.

While flying to Las Vegas one September day, I read a local paper that mentioned that the Southern Paiute people used to live in the desert region, but only a few still existed in small reservations today. When I got to the rental car facility, I overheard a conversation with a man telling his wife that "this place was crawlin' with Indians, but they're all gone now." I drove through the Valley of Fire State Park and walked up the stairs to view Atlatl Rock, a series of elaborate pictographs. Circles, snakes, people, rivers, animals, and other forms of life interact on a stunning wall of red rock (see figure 7.1). There is one image of a human throwing an atlatl, an ancient tool for hunting, hence its name. It's odd climbing up green metal stairs to view this rock art, and one wonders how the Paiute people used to access it and if they still do. The impression is given that this rock art represents cryptic symbols from an archaic, vanished people. In the state park interpretation signs, there is no mention that the Moapa Paiute Indian Reservation, established in 1873, is just thirty-five miles away. Hours later as I drive through Zion National Park, I stop at their visitor center to check out their interpretation of the local tribes. At a very impressive, ecologically designed visitor center, I read outdoor display panels about the history of inhabitation and settlement by Southern Paiute people in those deeply sculpted red and white canyons. There is one panel dedicated to mentioning that some Southern Paiute still exist today and work to preserve their traditions. Again, no mention of the numerous Paiute bands that still surround this national park. The next morning, as I pull into the Pipe Springs National Monument on the Kaibab Paiute Indian Reservation, I am greeted by a warm young woman in a park service uniform who asks, "Are you looking for Vivienne Jake?" "Yes," I reply, surprised this woman knows the intention of my visit. "Hi," she says, smiling brightly, "I'm her niece, and she lives down this road. She's expecting you." Family. Kin. Relations. About 250 people live on the Kaibab Paiute Indian Reservation. Everyone knows each other, and they certainly know Vivienne, who has worked on the tribal council, with the Environmental Protection Agency, with the Repatriation Committee, as a social worker, language advocate, salt song singer, and numerous other positions and roles.

The Kaibab band of Paiute are one of thirteen federally recognized Southern Paiute tribes that make up the Southern Paiute Nation, whose traditional territory spans parts of California, Arizona, Nevada, and Utah. Geographically, the Southern Paiute territory includes the Southern Great Basin desert, the Northern Colorado Plateau, the East Mojave Desert, and the San Juan-Colorado River drainage. The Kaibab Reservation in northern Arizona is 120,400 acres (see figure 7.2), a small fraction of land out of millions of acres of ancestral lands now owned and managed by private property owners, the National Park Service, state parks, U.S. Forest Service, and the Bureau of Land Management.

It was remarkable how many different stories I heard about the Southern Paiute while traveling to their Kaibab reservation lands.

I heard or read that the Southern Paiute didn't exist, that they did exist but only marginally, that they were "all gone," and that some had survived to today. The overall impression was that they are survivors, but still endangered. After taking in all of these mixed messages, I was especially happy to be invited to Kaibab Paiute land to assist in the recording of Vivienne Jake's oral history. It's one thing to hear stories *about* people; it's quite another to hear the stories directly from the people themselves, from individuals talking about their own personal, lived experiences. Hearing Vivienne discuss the sophisticated survival arts of the Southern Paiute, I wondered who in America, ethnically speaking, is really endangered.

At the beginning of the twenty-first century, thanks to indigenous scholars and revisionist historians, most of us realize that the stories we read or hear about American Indians are biased and often untrue—there are *his* stories, *her* stories, *their* stories, and *our* stories. Each of these types of stories represents specific perspectives through the lenses of gender, outsider, insider, colonizer, and colonized. When telling or hearing a story, I try to consider what is the purpose of the story and who has the right and responsibility to tell and hear it. This essay will examine the contemporary importance of Native American oral tradition in light of tribally initiated projects and explore the important and often overlooked connections between oral tradition, identity, and healing.

Native cultures around the world communicate through the oral tradition. Before colonization, stories were the primary pedagogical tool of Indian nations, whether sharing an account of a people's origins; describing how to gather plants for food or medicine, how to prepare for a puberty ceremony, when to plant corn or other crops; or teachings on ways to govern a village, clan, or nation. Today, these traditional stories, often called indigenous knowledge, are still told, though not as much as they used to be because the elders that know these old teachings and narratives are passing on and younger generations are not often hearing them, listening to them, or learning them. Thus, these traditional or preconquest stories of native life are endangered, and fewer and fewer people know them, remember them, or can retell them or teach them. Today, rather than hearing preconquest knowledge encoded in native narrative, or what some culture bearers prefer to simply call "teachings," a lot of native stories revolve around the effects of colonization: the boarding school experience, commodity foods, relocation to urban areas, troubles with the BIA and the allotment process, alcoholism, diabetes, AIM and Indian activism, loss of language and native foods, cross-cultural and intertribal relations, mixed-blood identity, and the challenge of maintaining indigenous traditions in a Western, industrial world. Of course, there's also the proverbial gossip of current events: who's marrying who, new babies and feasts, recent deaths, employment ups and down, casino wins and losses, new jokes, sports, and Indian politics. Stories span from the sacred to the profane, from the before worlds to today, from the individual to the tribal, from the human to the more-than-human. This ability to traverse such vast metaphorical territory in daily conversation is one of the most exciting aspects of verbal exchange within Native American communities. Anishinaabe writer Gerald Vizenor might call this imaginative, facile dialogue "trickster discourse," that is, "a wild venture in communal discourse, an uncertain humor that denies aestheticism, translation, and imposed representations."[1]

I want to avoid the comfortable trap of polemics by pointing out that I do not necessarily believe in an idealized "past" as opposed to a chaotic present or of a "traditional" way as opposed to a contemporary or postcolonial way. Yes, these distinctions exist, but as fluid representations depending on perspective and context. Many Western sociologists and psychologists have proposed various theories and models regarding Indian identity and often represent them in a linear way with the "Traditional Indian" on one end of the spectrum and the "Acculturated Indian" on the other end. According to this model, we, contemporary mixed-blood Native Americans, fall somewhere along this line depending on if we speak our language or not, whether we were raised on a reservation or not, whether we eat corn and wild rice or Big Macs, and many other factors. The problem with these linear models is obvious—they are overly simplistic. They beg the questions: Is it accurate, appropriate, or ethical to define a "traditional American Indian identity"? According to whose criteria? Which Tribe or era? Is describing an essential Indianness different from enforcing a stereotypical notion of primitiveness? Additionally, these linear models don't necessarily allow identity to change over time. Referring to American Indian literature, Vizenor states that "the process of literary annihilation would be checked only when Indian writers began representing their own culture."[2]

Likewise, identity annihilation would only be checked when Indian writers begin representing their own cultures and identities. One example of this reclamation of identity and culture is by the San Francisco Bay Area–based Muwekma Ohlone Tribe. They announce in conferences, publications, and federal hearings that they have survived the "politics of erasure" and are "back from extinction!"[3] So what kind of identity does an unrecognized urban tribe have after over two hundred years of identity annihilation by missions, governments, anthropologists, historians, and media? Clearly, their identity is not going to be based on an idea of an essential or traditional Indian-ness, yet they recognize themselves as authentic and demand to be recognized by others and the federal government as an American Indian nation. This example hopefully illustrates that Indian identity is far too complex and spirited to reduce and compartmentalize. Yet how do we still address the fact that many Indian elders are concerned that "there are no 'real' Indians left" or proclaim "our traditions are dying"? I've often heard modern technology and media being blamed for the decline in native traditions. Some native youth would rather watch TV or play a video game than learn how to weave a basket or prepare for a naming ceremony. But there are many native youth who like to do both, like recording rez rap on a digital mini-disc recorder while shaking a gourd rattle and singing contemporary urban lyrics in Cahuilla. Technology and media have certainly changed and harmed many Indian traditions. But today, indigenous communities are using this same media technology (TV, radio, film) to tell their *own* stories and renew cultural knowledge and practices.[4]

Within and without native communities, there exist real experiences and perceptions that some Native People are more in touch with their traditions than others. There are several younger generations (born during and after the '60s) of mixed-bloods who want to learn and restore the Native traditions of their ancestors (languages, foods, names, customs, etc.), despite having grown up in an urban industrial world. To emphasize the importance of Indian identity and these apparent dilemmas, Native sociologist Joseph Gone examines Indian identity as "who you are" and "what you do."[5] He supports and elaborates on a dynamic, "empty center" model of Indian identity developed by medical anthropologist Theresa O'Nell.[6] The "Traditional Indian" is in the center ("bull's-eye") of a series of con-

centric circles moving out to the periphery, where the "Acculturated Indian" is located. Unlike in the linear model, an individual can
move from one identity circle to another in this dynamic, discursive
model. Even after extensive interviews with Indian elders on the Fort
Belknap Indian reservation where Gone is from, he also supports this
idea that authentic Indian identity is extremely subtle and difficult to
locate. The center of this model is therefore empty. All of us, including Indian grandmothers and grandfathers on reservations, move
back and forth on this dynamic model of identity. One of O'Nell
and Gone's main points is that identity is changeable depending
on social context. So an urban mixed-blood telling a "story" about
relocation would be "traditional" in the context of an all-white class-
room, but the same person telling the same story to a group of elders
at a tribal senior citizen center would be considered "acculturated."
A sixty-five-year-old tribal member giving a ceremonial welcoming
address at a sobriety powwow would be "traditional," but when
in the roundhouse for a healing ceremony with everyone, except
this person, speaking the old dialect of their mother tongue, they
would be considered "acculturated." The "empty center" model
allows us to change, adapt, and be more fluid with how we express
and identify ourselves. This is more in touch with Vizenor's notion
of trickster identity that "is itself a subversion of the Western mode
of classification, resisting singularity (and therefore becoming in
Vizenor's work a perfect metaphor for the mixedblood)."[7] Trickster
identity allows us to be in the center, as well as the periphery. "Trickster mediates between supposed contradictory forces or elements
by retaining aspects of both, or by revealing them to be co-existing
parts of one whole, interconnected, often indistinguishable elements
of the one."[8] Whether a linear, discursive, or trickster type of identity, how do these models inform our understanding of the importance of the oral tradition in Native America? Gone and others have
concluded that identity and narrative are inextricably intertwined.
Gone continues to argue that "the kind of communicative interac-
tion best suited to the construction of cultural identity is the recount-
ing of past personal narratives to particular audiences for particular
purposes."[9] Anishinaabe scholar Lawrence Gross also supports this
essential connection between oral tradition and cultural identity, "as
long as the sacred stories of a people remain viable, their religion
and culture can remain functional."[10]

Most of human language revolves around the power of words, speech, story, narrative to make, report on, or re-create reality, depending on your philosophical worldview. The Sapir-Whorf hypothesis, for example, claims that human language shapes cognition to such a degree that it creates the reality we think we're reporting on. Whether one subscribes to this hypothesis or not, it is clear that language and thought are closely related and strongly affect our perceptions of ourselves, each other, and the world around us. Therefore, a better understanding of our languages and the stories we tell (and don't tell) will affect our sense of identity. Concomitantly, our sense of identity (who we are and what we do) is related to our sense of health and well-being. Native American language preservation and the documentation of oral tradition are then important goals and activities in and of themselves, but they also provide real and potential doorways for cultural recovery and individual and collective healing.

Through community activism and applied research, I have been privileged and honored to assist Native communities in recording their own stories for their own purposes. These stories are based in the oral tradition and therefore are unwritten according to the Western concept of language. They may have been "written" by ancestors or other spirit mentors in the land itself as geologic features, petroglyphs or pictographs, birchbark scrolls, winter count hide paintings, or other symbols and signs. Fewer and fewer Native elders can read the language of the land and ancestral markings like this, but many still can and are teaching these advanced skills to others.[11] Also, some younger folks are gaining their own visions, through art, singing, weaving, digital storytelling, gardening, and other work, and are able to understand these special signs.

Even though anthropologists, ethnologists, linguists, and early explorers and missionaries have been trying to gather and collect Native American oral traditions for a couple of hundred years, a lot of Native stories and teachings have not been recorded by outsiders. Consequently, these undocumented stories have not been subject to as much misinterpretation and misappropriation as "collected" stories have been. A lot of traditional cultural knowledge and practices have been "lost" because they have not been recorded by outsiders. Many see this as a tragedy because the rest of the world did not have the opportunity to learn about these different ways of perceiving and living in the world. Also, these Native communities did not have the opportunity to share their unique perspectives and understanding (their side of the story) with the outsider. But many Native elders explicitly chose, and continue to choose, *not* to share their cultural knowledge with outsiders because of the justified concern of being exploited, ridiculed, misappropriated, dissected, and commodified. Besides that, many elders feel that this knowledge never really disappears or goes extinct; it simply goes dormant in the earth until someone is ready to be responsible to that knowledge again. When that person is ready for that specific knowledge, it will emerge from the cultural landscape and find its home in that individual's mind/heart/body/spirit.

I acknowledge the reasons for this position and completely support Native Peoples' decision to keep traditional knowledge internal among their own people. This is one of the only ways to protect the sanctity of traditional knowledge, assert cultural privacy, and, from a Western perspective, remain in control of one's cultural and intellectual property rights. This position of cultural privacy is an important way to assert cultural sovereignty. Having said that, I also greatly value and respect those Native nations, tribes, bands, families, elders, and individuals who decide to share specific stories and knowledges for specific purposes. The Kogi people of Colombia, for example, felt that it was time, in the late '80s, to share their unique worldview with "younger brother," the outside world, to try to prevent global catastrophe and sustain their way of life.[12] Other Native Peoples, from Northern Paiute leader Sarah Winnemucca[13] to Lakota holy man Lame Deer,[14] have decided to share certain aspects of their traditional knowledge and practices because they felt it was important to educate the outsider about their unique way of life.

Regarding the process of transmitting cultural knowledge, it is ironic that I have heard many Native elders say that outsiders are more interested in their cultural knowledge than their own tribal members. It seems ironic, but with a deeper investigation, there are predictable patterns of denial, wounding, and forgetting that characterize many Native American communities and others who are survivors of holocaust. One of the many destructive consequences of attempted genocide is Post-traumatic Stress Disorder (PTSD). After centuries of conquest, Native communities respond with individual and collective PTSD. This trauma has tragically been ignored by most Indian health care providers until quite recently.[15] Historical trauma, unaddressed, is passed on from one generation to the next. Ongoing trauma and oppression coming from federal, state, and local government; religion; education; economics; and society at large become internalized. Oppressed people begin to oppress themselves. This highly relevant, important topic is beyond the scope of this paper, but it is important to note that it is at play with all of these issues of ethnography, identity, oral tradition, and cultural health.

So how is it that I find myself, an Anishinaabe/Métis second-generation urban relocatee, telling the story of how I work with members of the Southern Paiute Nation to protect and restore the histories and teachings of their rich oral tradition?

For the past twelve years I have managed the Cultural Conservancy, a grassroots indigenous-rights nonprofit organization whose mission is to preserve and revitalize indigenous cultures and their ancestral lands. At the request of tribes, indigenous communities, and individuals, we work on a variety of environmental and cultural restoration projects. Through research, education, and advocacy we have protected Native American sacred sites, Native plant gathering places, and the diverse cultural ecologies and practices of place-based Native Peoples. In 1998, we partnered with environmental- and indigenous-rights activist Philip M. Klasky to create the Storyscape Project. This project emerged, in large part, out of Klasky's successful efforts to assist the Fort Mojave Indian Tribe; Chemehuevi Indian Tribe; and Quechan, Cocopah, and Colorado River Indian Tribes in stopping the proposal for a nuclear waste dump at Ward Valley, California, on land considered sacred by the tribes. We conducted research into traditional Mojave songs to help establish aboriginal territory and assert the cultural and religious significance of Ward Valley (*Silyaye Ahease*) as part of a legal strategy to protect the land. From that important environmental justice work, it became even clearer that the documentation of traditional Native stories and songs is an important way to lay claim to ancestral lands.

Oral histories and narratives not only give personal identity to individuals; they can give ecological identity and unity to a people. For too long these voices of unity have been silenced, erased, and marginalized to keep Native People divided and conquered by coercive government and private interests. Maori scholar Linda Smith says divide and conquer still exists because sadly it still works. It takes vision and leadership to decolonize from these destructive patterns and develop unity among diverse peoples. I feel fortunate to have met two such Southern Paiute leaders who feel that it is time to share some of their oral tradition and survival arts with other Native People and the outside world to create greater harmony through intergenerational healing.

In 2001 the Cultural Conservancy was asked to assist Kaibab Paiute elder Vivienne Jake and Chemehuevi leader Matthew Leivas, codirectors of the Salt Song Project of the Native American Land Conservancy, in the audio recording of their historic salt songs. Digital audio recordings were completed, and all of the Paiute bands and singers have copies to use for their own purposes. The Southern Paiute Nation owns the copyright to these historic recordings. The Cultural Conservancy simply provided a service, in the form of audio recording and production, to accomplish their goal of creating audio tools for young Paiute to learn these invaluable songs. The purpose of the Southern Paiute salt songs is to heal the living and the dead and outline a sacred journey both on this earth and in the spirit world. Prophecies in the oral tradition describe a time when these songs will be shared with other tribes and the outside world for that specific purpose: to heal the living and the dead and outline a sacred journey both on this earth and in the spirit world. Paiute elder Vivienne Jake feels that this is the time to share the meaning and importance of these sacred songs and the stories they contain: "These songs are very powerful. They are the songs that are going to unite our people again. It's going to be a spiritual awakening of the Native American people, especially other Paiute people. It has to happen. It has been prophesized. How do you stop prophecy? You can't stop prophecy."[16]

Today, according to Vivienne Jake and Matt Leivas, it is again time to document and pay tribute to the sites along the geographic trail sung about in the salt songs. This has been done by tribal elders and singers throughout time and by the well-known ethnographer Carobeth Laird in her classic book on *The Chemehuevis*.[17] Additionally, anthropologist Richard Stoffle discusses the importance of the Southern Paiute songscapes and storyscapes.[18] Stoffle explains,

Figure 7.1.   Atlatl Rock, Valley of Fire State Park, Nevada.

"Were one to pass along the path of the story, the landscape would be marked with story or song points. Moving from point to point permits a living person to physically reenact and directly experience the story or song."[19]

These ethnographers obviously gained their knowledge from Southern Paiute tribal members who continue the salt song tradition. As a way to pass on the traditions she carries, Vivienne Jake asked me to assist her in recording her oral history. She shares stories from traditional times as well as ones that reflect the impacts of colonization on her people. Vivienne is recording and writing her personal stories primarily for her own family and tribe, and some of her stories, like her experiences in boarding school and the importance of the salt songs, will be shared with a wider audience for education and healing. According to many Southern Paiute, the salt songs need to be documented to educate young Paiute members about their meaning, significance, history, locations, and purpose. The prophecies of the salt songs are extremely important, and

Figure 7.2.   Kaibab Paiute Indian Reservation, Arizona.

Vivienne plans to organize singing ceremonies at boarding schools and undocumented massacre sites to help heal the Paiute dead who have not had their proper right of passage.

The beginning of this vision was accomplished in the spring of 2004 when a group of Southern Paiute organized a "Sing" at the Sherman Indian School cemetery in Riverside, California, to honor and release the spirits of dozens of Indian children who died at the boarding school and never came home. One spring day in May the Cultural Conservancy received calls from Matthew Leivas and Vivienne Jake telling us they were going to be performing the salt songs at the Sherman cemetery. They requested that we and our media team join them and film the historic event. We scrambled around for four days finding the best equipment and camera people we could, and five of us traveled to Riverside to meet with Matt and Vivienne and the rest of the salt song singers and family supporters. In an open field between already dry southern California hills and the edge of Riverside suburbia, Southern Paiute salt song singers, their friends and family, and other native supporters gathered in

Figure 7.3. Vivienne Jake (Kaibab Paiute) and Matthew Leivas (Chemehuevi), Salt Song Project Directors, reviewing archival material at the Sherman Indian School Museum, Riverside, California, May 2004.

ceremony at the small fenced-in cemetery to sing for these children. The singers decided to only sing the last four songs of the 142-song cycle as a way to protect the sacredness of the songs and yet still be recorded. In this way, the living voices of the salt song singers honored the children, the land, and the voices of their people. In their view, the songs provide a spiritual trail so that the spirits of the dead may find their way to the other side of the chasm, a chasm literally and symbolically characterized as a Grand Canyon between life and death. The voices of the Southern Paiute salt singers praying in their native tongue awaken the rich life and kinship they have with their relatives. Through their songs, a healing resonance is created between the ancestors and the present community. This type of intergenerational healing is absolutely necessary for American Indian peoples today and demonstrates the power of the oral tradition for cultural survival and native renewal.

The Salt Song Project and the Cultural Conservancy just completed a twenty-minute documentary film, *The Salt Song Trail—Bringing Creation Back Together*, about the salt songs, their trail, and the healing ceremony at Sherman Indian School cemetery.[20] Through community-based projects such as this, Native People and the partners they choose can address the devastating consequences of genocide, colonization, and internalized oppression and develop creative approaches that can help facilitate collective healing in both the seen and unseen worlds.

Notes

Melissa K. Nelson can be contacted at: Melissa K. Nelson, Assistant Professor, American Indian Studies, College of Ethnic Studies, San Francisco State University, 1600 Holloway Drive, San Francisco, CA 94132. This chapter was prepared in collaboration with and special thanks to Vivienne Jake, who can be contacted at: Vivienne Jake, P.O. Box 68, Fredonia, AZ 85344.

1. Gerald Vizenor, *The Trickster of Liberty: Tribal Heirs to a Wild Baronage* (Minneapolis: University of Minnesota Press, 1988), ix–x.

2. Vizenor, *The Trickster of Liberty*.

3. Lowell Bean, *The Ohlone Past and Present* (Menlo Park, CA: Ballena Press, 1994).

4. See Emily Getz, "Indigenous People Bridging the Digital Divide," *Cultural Survival* 29, no. 2 (Summer 2005).

5. Joseph Gone, "Mental Health, Wellness, and the Quest for an Authentic American Indian Identity," in *No Longer Forgotten: Addressing the mental health needs of urban Indians*, edited by T. Witko (Washington, DC: American Psychological Association, forthcoming).

6. Theresa O'Nell, *Disciplined Hearts: History, Identity and Depression in an American Indian Community* (Los Angeles: University of California Press, 1996).

7. Kimberly Blaeser, *Gerald Vizenor: Writing in the Oral Tradition* (Norman: University of Oklahoma Press, 1996), 138.

8. Blaeser, *Gerald Vizenor*, 139.

9. Gone, "Mental Health," 15.

10. Lawrence Gross, "Cultural Sovereignty and Native American Hermeneutics in the Interpretation of the Sacred Stories of the Anishinaabe," *Wicazo Sa Review* 18, no. 2 (Fall 2003).

11. Louise Erdrich, *Books and Islands in Ojibwe Country* (Washington, DC: National Geographic Press, 2003).

12. See Alan Ereira's film and book, *The Message from the Heart of the World: Elder Brother's Warning* (Mystic Fire Video, 1990) and *The Heart of the World* (London: J. Cape, 1990), respectively.

13. Sarah Winnemucca Hopkins, *Life Among the Piutes: Their Wrongs and Claims* (New York: G. P. Putnam's Sons, 1883).

14. John Lame Deer and Richard Erdoes, *Lame Deer, Seeker of Visions* (New York: Washington Square Press, 1994).

15. Fortunately, today there are more Indian psychologists and doctors who are addressing historical trauma and internalized oppression. See Eduardo and Bonnie Duran's *Native American Postcolonial Psychology* (New York: SUNY Press, 1995).

16. Interview with Vivienne Jake.

17. Carobeth Laird, *The Chemehuevis (What's New in Plant Physiology)* (Banning, CA: Malki Museum Press, 1976).

18. Richard Stoffle, David B. Halmo, and Diane E. Austin, "Cultural Landscapes and Traditional Cultural Properties: A Southern Paiute View of the Grand Canyon and Colorado River," *American Indian Quarterly* 21, no. 2 (Spring 1997): 229–249.

19. Stoffle, Halmo, and Austin, "Cultural Landscapes and Traditional Cultural Properties."

20. The film is available at www.nativeland.org or 415-561-6594.

8

In the Spirit of Crazy Horse

Winona LaDuke

> The purposeful use and appropriation of another ascertainable person's name or likeness in an insulting and disparaging manner without consent or permission of the lawful owner of said name or his heirs and especially in the commercial exploitation for financial gain in association with a product which has proved so deadly to Indian people, are despicable and disparaging invasions of privacy and are egregious violations of Lakota customary law protecting the spiritual, personal, social, and cultural importance of an individual's name to an individual and his family during his life and his spirit and reputation, along with those of his relations, after his life so as to amount to disparagement and defamation of both the individual and the group.[1]

On April 26, 2001, something rather remarkable happened. A beer company apologized. John W. Stroh III traveled to Mission, South Dakota, to the home of Tasunke Witko (Crazy Horse) Tiosapaye and issued a formal apology for his company, Stroh Brewery, and its relationship to a beer brewing company that had produced Crazy Horse Malt Liquor. In a moving ceremony, Stroh announced the gift of seven thoroughbred horses, thirty-two Pendleton blankets, thirty-two braids of sweet grass, and thirty-two twists of tobacco as the settlement to the Crazy Horse estate—all culturally significant items and all items requested by the Tasunke Witko estate as "relief" in the case filed in the Rosebud Sioux Tribal Court.

The racehorses were for each state, territory, or Nation in which said products had been distributed and offered for sale. Those items, as well as a formal letter of apology to the family, began a reconciliation process with the Tiosapaye; Seth Big Crow, representing the family, called the settlement "a victory for all Native Americans."[2]

Crazy Horse is considered to be one of the greatest leaders and military strategists of all time, largely responsible for the battles against Fetterman, Major Baker, and General Crook, as well as one of the leaders of the Battle of the Little Big Horn. He was born around 1842 on Rapid Creek; his mother was the sister of Spotted Tail. His lineage included Lakota from the Brule, Minnecoujou, and Oglala, as well as Cheyenne. He was called Curly, it is said, for many years because his hair and skin were a lighter color of brown than many of his relatives. He is said to have dressed plainly, his hair wrapped in beaver pelt strips, and adornments, with the exception of a rock which hung from his ear, were said to be simple.

He lived in a time of great challenge for the Lakota. Diseases had arrived into the region; smallpox was taking family members like his very own young daughter. In the time of strife, many Oglalas came to follow him; his power was considered to be very great. It is also said that this power was the source of envy for others and caused fear in the U.S. military. His assassination was orchestrated on September 5, 1877, at Fort Robinson. A soldier killed him with a bayonet as he was held by two Oglalas who had turned against him. As he passed on, his two relatives Worm and Touch the Clouds stood by in mourning. He passed to the spirit world. A hundred and twenty five years later, his presence remains through debates over the commercialization of his image and name.[3] So it was that in September of 1877, as Tasunke Witko—also known as Crazy Horse—lay dying at Fort Robinson, he spoke to his family. His dying instructions included a request that he be buried in a secret location and that they never speak of him to non-Native people in the future.

For generations the Tasunke Witko Tiosapaye kept that promise to their ancestor; but in 1993, Mr. Seth H. Big Crow, SR, received permission from his family (Tiosapaye) and subsequently from Rosebud Sioux Tribal Court, to assume the legal authority to act on behalf of the estate of his great-grandfather. The Rosebud Tribal Court ruled in the administrative appointment that "the estate included, but is not limited to, a personal property right regarding the descendant's name, which embraces such right so as to govern and protect the use of said descendant's name, particularly with regard to misappropriation and commercial exploitation of said name under the law of the Rosebud Sioux Tribe and any other applicable laws."[4]

It is not as if the name has not been heard in public before. After all, bars, horses, a line of clothing (JC Penney and Liz Claiborne) all use the name Crazy Horse. But perhaps the most offensive was the use of the name by a beer company. It was the brainchild of two Italian American businessmen, John Ferolito and Dom Vultaggio, both from Brooklyn, New York. These two men, who a decade before had been driving and delivering beer and soda trucks in New York City, conceptualized a "Family of American Original" beverages. They would produce the beverages through their family firm, the Hornell Brewing Company. The businessmen hoped to sell to upscale domestic markets and introduce a new line of premium liquors to an overseas market.[5]

Although Hornell Brewing Company appeared to most as a beer company in itself, Hornell is, in fact, according to Gough, "merely a paper corporation."[6] By simply obtaining the legal rights to this corporate name, they attained the instant legal identity of a long-established brewing business. "None of these companies own any brewing facilities and are invested primarily in label designs placed upon products brewed under contract by various large national breweries, such as Heileman and Stroh."[7] The company received additional criticism for its Midnight Dragon Malt Liquor, which featured a woman clad in a slinky red dress and garter drinking from a beer bottle through a straw, with the tag line, "I could suck on this all night." That beer became the target of protests by women's groups. The Midnight Dragon Malt Liquor was similarly targeted toward the African American community. That liquor was pulled off the market after protests primarily by black churches and social activist groups. It was a few years later, in March of 1992, that the exact same malt liquor was reintroduced as Crazy Horse Malt Liquor.[8]

It is not only the problem of the use of the name of Crazy Horse by the brewery, but, additionally, it is the significance of the impact that alcohol has had on the Lakota and other indigenous cultures. Liquor has been described by some as "one of the earliest chemical warfare agents used against Indians by Europeans and later fur traders and settlers to disable Native intelligence and begin the feeding frenzy on what the European saw as his innate destiny to possess."[9]

Defense of Spirit

Lakota Wo'ope, or Lakota Customary Law, is the backbone of Lakota culture and covers pretty much how the people should behave toward one other. It violates the custom of Lakota Wo'ope to use someone's name after they are dead. Robert Gough, attorney for the Tasunke Witko Tiosapaye, explains in an interview that "it was this principle which was the underlying basis for the lawsuit that was filed by the estate of Tasunke Witko Tiosapaye in August of 1993 in the Rosebud Sioux Tribal Court against the Crazy Horse Malt Liquor Company for the defamation of the spirit of Crazy Horse."[10]

The use of cultural custom and the right of the family to determine how Crazy Horse's name would be used was the first facet of Gough's legal strategy to get the beers pulled. The case has since gone through various manifestations, beginning with Rosebud Sioux Tribal Court, where the plaintiffs sought to have tribal law determined and announced by the court itself. As Gough explains, "The Estate's legal strategy involves in an invocation and application of culturally-based Lakota tribal law as may be provided under applicable United States federal law and procedure." In his decision, Rosebud Tribal Judge Whiting held that "the estate of Crazy Horse holds the exclusive rights of publicity in the name and persona of Crazy Horse, specifically stating that the plaintiffs have a postmortem right of publicity in the good name of Crazy Horse."[11]

The second facet of the legal strategy dealt with federal regulations as they relate to the issue of trademark and copyright laws. This particular argument was complicated by the fact that neither patents nor copyright laws apply to people's names. In the case, Stroh settled under tribal law, which is what he wanted to do all along, just settle.

Perhaps in a moment of sensitivity, it appears that even large oil companies are getting the sensibilities of cultural property rights that were so difficult for the beer breweries to understand.

For example, in 2002 the president of British Petroleum made a trip to the Rosebud Reservation. It appears that the corporation had named its largest oil find in the Gulf of Mexico "Crazy Horse." The leadership of the company got wind of the Lakota concerns, and, as Gough explains, "although it took a little time, they decided to officially change the name of the company. They actually brought a commemoration plaque up and presented it along with some sweet grass and tobacco during a meeting that they had with the descendants of Crazy Horse."[12]

To the Rosebud Lakota and the Tasunke Witko Tiosapaye, "all of these are recognitions of the right of the tribe and the estate to control the use of the name, Crazy Horse." And it is also a recognition, as Gough surmises, "of tribal law" and an affirmation of the sovereign legal rights of indigenous nations throughout North America. For those who've misused and inappropriately represented the spirit of Crazy Horse's name and that of his people, there is something to be said for the words *I'm sorry*.

Notes

1. Count I of the Estate Tribal Court complaint, in the case of Crazy Horse Malt Liquor, 1997.

2. Heidi Bell Gease, "Stroh Apologizes for Crazy Horse Brew," *Rapid City Journal*, April 26, 2001.

3. Mari Sandoz, *Crazy Horse: Strange Man of the Oglalas: A Biography* (Lincoln: University of Nebraska Press, 1961).

4. Bob Gough, interview from *Native America Calling*, September 3, 2002.

5. Gough, interview from *Native America Calling*, 17.

6. Gough, interview from *Native America Calling*.

7. Gough, interview from *Native America Calling*, 17.

8. Statement of Seth Big Crow, Crazy Horse Defense Project website, www.crazyhorsedefense.org/, accessed October 2002.

9. Patricia D. Mail and Saundra Johnson, "Boozing, Sniffing and Toking: An Overview of Past, Present and Future of Substance Abuse by American Indians," *American Indian and Alaskan Native Mental Health Research Journal of the National Center* 5, no. 2 (1993): 16.

10. Gough, interview from *Native America Calling*, 8.

11. www.crazyhorsedefense.org, 2002.

12. Gough, interview from *Native America Calling*.

III

CONTESTATION AND MIXED-RACE IDENTITY

9

Chicana Feminism:
In the Tracks of "the"
Native Woman

Norma Alarcón

As Spain prepared to celebrate the quincentenary of "the discovery," contemporary Chicanas were deliberating on the force of the significations of that event. It took almost four hundred years for the territory we call Mexico to acquire a cohesive national identity and sovereignty. Centuries passed before the majority of the inhabitants were able to call themselves Mexican citizens. As a result, on the Mexican side of the designation Mexican American, Chicanas rethink their involvement in the capitalist neocolonization of the population of Mexican descent in the United States (Barrera et al. 1972).

In the 1960s, armed with a post–Mexican American critical consciousness, some people of Mexican descent in the United States recuperated, appropriated, and recodified the term *Chicano* to form a new political class (Acuña 1981; Munoz 1989). Initially, the new appellation left the entrenched (middle-class) intellectuals mute because it emerged from oral usage in the working-class communities. In effect, the name measured the distance between the excluded and the few who had found a place for themselves in Anglo-America. The new Chicano political class began to work on the compound name, eager to redefine the economic, racial, cultural, and political position of the people. The appropriation and recodification of the term *Chicano* from the oral culture was a stroke of insight precisely because it unsettled all of the identities conferred

119

by previous historical accounts. The apparently well-documented terrains of the dyad Mexico/United States were repositioned and reconfigured through the inclusion of the excluded in the very interiority of culture, knowledge, and the political economy. Thus, the demand for Chicano/a history became a call for the recovery and rearticulation of the record to include the stories of race/class relations of the silenced, against whom the very notions of being Mexican or not-Mexican, being American or not-American, being a citizen or not a citizen had been constructed. In brief, the call for the story of Chicana/os has not turned out to be a "definite" culture, as some dreamed. Rather, the term itself, in body and mind, has become a critical site of "definitiveness," and hegemonic tendencies are placed in question.

Although the formation of the new political Chicano class has been dominated by men, Chicana feminists have intervened from the beginning. The early Chicana intervention is available in the serials and journals mushroomed in tandem with the alternative press in the United States in the 1960s and 1970s. Unfortunately, much of that early work by Chicanas often goes unrecognized, which is indicative of the process of erasure and exclusion of raced ethnic women within a patriarchal cultural and political economy. In the 1980s, however, there was a reemergence of Chicana writers and scholars who have not only repositioned the Chicano political class through the feminist register but who have joined forces with an emergent women-of-color political class that has national and international implications (McLaughlin 1991).

The United States in the 1980s was, according to the Reagan administration, the decade of the Hispanic—a neoconservative move assisted by the U.S. Census Bureau (Giménez 1989) and the mass media, to homogenize all people of Latin American descent and occlude their heterogeneous histories of resistance to domination—in other words, the counterhistories to invasions and conquests. At the same time, in the 1980s, a more visible Chicana feminist intervention had given new life to a stalled Chicano movement (Rojas 1989). In fact, in the United States, this appears to be the case among most raced ethnic minorities. By including feminist and gender analysis into emergent political class, Chicanas are reconfiguring the meaning of cultural and political resistance and redefining the jointure of the term Mexican American (Moraga and Anzaldúa 1981; Alarcón 1989, 1990).

To date, most writers of Mexican descent refuse to give up the term *Chicana*. Despite the social reaccommodation of many as Hispanics or Mexican Americans, it is the consideration of the excluded evoked by the name Chicana that provides the position for multiple cultural critiques: between and within, inside and outside, centers and margins. Working-class and peasant women, perhaps the "last colony," as a recent book announces (Mies et al. 1989), are most keenly aware of this. As a result, when many a writer of such racialized cultural history explores her identity, a reflectory and refractory position is depicted. In the words of Gloria Anzaldúa:

> She has this fear
> that she has no names
> that she has many names
> that she doesn't know her names
> She has this fear
> that she's an image
> that comes and goes
> clearing and darkening
> the fear that she's the dreamwork inside someone else's skull . . .
> She has this fear that if she digs into herself
> she won't find anyone
> that when she gets "there"
> she won't find her notches on the trees . . .
> She has this fear that she won't find the way back. (1987: 43)

The quest for a true self and identity, which was the initial desire of many writers involved in the Chicano movement in the late 1960s and early 1970s, has given way to the realization that there is no fixed identity. "I," or "She" as observed by Anzaldúa, is composed of multiple layers without necessarily yielding an uncontested "origin." In the words of Trinh T. Minh-ha, "Things may be said to be what they are, not exclusively in relation to what was and what will be (they should not solely be seen as clusters chained together by the temporal sequence of cause and effect), but also in relation to each other's immediate presences and to themselves as non/presences" (1989: 94). Thus, the name Chicana, in the present, is the name of resistance that enables cultural and political points of departure and thinking through the multiple migrations and dislocations of women of "Mexican" descent. The name Chicana is not a name that women (or men) are born to or with, as is often the case with Mexican, but rather is consciously and critically assumed and serves as a point of departure for dismantling historical conjunctures of crisis, confusion, political and ideological conflict, and contradictions of the simultaneous effects of having "no names," having "many names," not "know(ing) her names," and being someone else's "dreamwork." Digging into the historically despised dark (prieto) body, in strictly psychological terms, may get her to the bare bones and marrow, but she may not "find the way back" to writing her embodied histories. The idea of pluralized historical bodies is proposed with respect to the multiple racial constructions of the body since "the discovery": to name a few, indigenous (evoking the extant as well as extinct tribes), criolla, morisca, loba, cambuja, barcina, coyota, samba, mulatta, china, chola. The contemporary assumption of *mestizaje* (hybridism) in the Mexican nation-making process was intended to racially colligate a heterogeneous population that was not European. On the American side of the compound, *mestizas* are nonwhite, thus further reducing the cultural and historical experience of Chicanas. However, the mestiza concept is always already bursting its boundaries. While some have "forgotten" the mestiza genealogy, others claim as indigenous Black or Asian ones as well. In short, the body, certainly in the past five hundred years in the Americas, has been always already racialized. As tribal "ethnicities" are broken down by conquest and colonizations, bodies are often multiply racialized and dislocated as if they had no other contents. The effort to recontextualize the processes recovers, speaks for, or gives voice to women on the bottom of a historically hierarchical economic and political structure (Spivak 1988).

It is not coincidental that as Chicana writers reconstruct the multiple names of the mestiza and Indian, social scientists and historians find them in the segmented labor force or in the grip of armed struggles. In fact, most of these women have been (and continue to be) the surplus sources of cheap labor in the field, the canneries, the maquiladora border industries, and domestic services. The effort to pluralize the racialized body by redefining part of their experience through the reappropriation of "the" Native women on Chicana feminists terms marked one of the first assaults on male-centered cultural nationalism on the one hand (Alarcón 1989), and patriarchal political economy on the other (Melville 1980; Mora et al. 1980; Cordova et al. 1986; Ruiz and Tiano 1987; Zavella 1987).

The Native woman has many names also—Coatlicue, Cihuacoátl, Ixtacihúatl, and so on. In fact, one has only to consult the dictionary of *Mitologia Nahuátl*, for example, to discover many more that have not been invoked. For many writers, the point is not so much to recover a lost "utopia" or the "true" essence of our being, though, of course, there are those among us who long for the "lost origins," as well as those who feel a profound spiritual kinship with the "lost"—a spirituality whose resistant political implications must not be underestimated, but refocused for feminist change (Allen 1988). The most relevant point in the present is to understand how a pivotal indigenous portion of the mestiza past may represent a collective female experience as well as "the mark of the beast" within us—the maligned and abused indigenous woman (Anzaldúa 1987: 43). By invoking the "dark Beast" within and without, which has forced us to deny, the cultural and psychic dismemberment that is linked to imperialist racist and sexist practices is brought into focus. These practices are not a thing of the past either. One only has to recall the contemporary massacres of the Indian population in Guatemala, for example, or the continuous "democratic" interventionist tactics in Central and South America, which often result in the violent repression of the population.

It is not surprising, then, that many Chicana writers explore their racial and sexual experiences in poetry, narrative, essay, testimony, and autobiography through the evocation of indigenous figures. This is a strategy that Gloria Anzaldúa uses and calls "la herencia de Coatlicue/the Coatlicue state." The "state" is, paradoxically, an ongoing process, a continuous effort of consciousness to make "sense" of something; she has to "cross over," kicking a hole out of the old boundaries of the self and slipping under or over, dragging the old skin along, stumbling over it (Anzaldúa 1987: 48–49). The contemporary subject-in-process is not just what Hegel would have us call the *Aufhebung*—that is, the effort to unify consciousness "is provided within a radical recomprehension of the totality" (Warren 1984: 37)—as tenuously, Chicana's consciousness, which is too readily viewed as representing "postmodern fragmenting identities," entails not only Hegel's *Aufhebung* with respect to Chicanas' immediate personal subjectivity as raced and sexed bodies, but also an understanding of all past negations as communitarian subjects in a doubled relation to cultural recollection, and remembrance, and to our contemporary presence and non/presence in the sociopolitical and cultural milieu. All of which together enables both individual and group Chicana positions previously "empty" of meaning to emerge as one who has to "make sense" of it all from the bottom through the recodification of the Native woman. As such, the so-called postmodern decentered subject, a decentralization that implies diverse, multiply constructed subjects and historical conjunctures, insofar as she desires liberation, must move toward provisional solidarities, especially through social movements. In this fashion, one may recognize the endless production of differences to destabilize group or collective identities on the one hand, and the need for group solidarities to overcome oppression through and understanding of the mechanisms at work on the other (McLaughlin 1991; Kauffman 1990).

The strategic invocation and recodification of "the" Native woman in the present has the effect of conjoining the historical repression of the "noncivilized" dark woman—which continues to operate through "regulative psychobiographies" of good and evil women such as that of Guadalupe, Malinche, Llorona, and many others—with the present moment of speech that counters such repressions (Spivak 1988: 227). It is worthwhile to remember that the historical founding moment of the construction of mestiza(s) subjectivity entails the rejection and denial of the dark Indian Mother as Indian, which has compelled women often to collude in silence against themselves, and to actually deny the Indian position even as that position is visually stylized and represented in the making of the fatherland. Within these blatant contradictions the overvaluation of European-ness is constantly at work. Thus, Mexico constructs its own ideological version of the notorious Anglo-American "melting pot," under the sign of mestizo(a). The unmasking, however, becomes possible for Chicanas as they are put through the crisis of the Anglo-American experience where ("melting-pot") whiteness, not mestizaje, has been constructed as the Absolute Idea of Goodness and Value in the Americas; then, the Native woman as ultimate sign of potential reproduction of *barbarie* (savagery) has served as the sign of consensus for most others, men and women. Women, under penalty of the double bind charge of "betrayal" of the fatherland (in the future sense) and the mother tongues (in the past sense), are often compelled to acquiesce with the "civilizing" new order in male terms. Thus, for example, the "rights" of women in Nicaragua disappear vis-à-vis the "democratizing" forces, notwithstanding Sandinista intensions (Molyneux 1985). In this scenario, to speak at all, then, "the" Native woman has to legitimize her position by becoming a "mother" in hegemonic patriarchal terms, which is near impossible to do unless she is "married" or racially "related" to the right men (Hurtado 1989). As a result, the contemporary challenge to the multiple negations and rejections of the Native racialized woman in the Americas is like few others.

For Chicanas, the consideration of the ideological constructions of the "noncivilized" dark woman brings into view a most sobering reference point: the overwhelming majority of the workers in maquiladoras, for example, are mestizas who have been forcefully subjected to not only the described processes but to many others that await disentanglement. Many of those workers are "single," unprotected within a cultural order that has required the masculine protection of women to ensure their "decency," indeed to ensure that they are "civilized" in sexual and racial terms. In fact, as Spivak and others have suggested, "the new army of 'permanent casual' labor working below the minimum wage . . . [are] these women [who today] represent the international neo-colonial subject paradigmatically" (Spivak 1988: 223). These woman (and some men), who were subjected to the Hispanic New World "feudal mode of power" (which in Mexico gave way to the construction of mestizo nationalism) and who were subjected to an Anglo-American "feudal mode of power" in the isolation of migrant worker camps and exchange labor (which in the United States gave rise to Chicano cultural nationalism of the 1960s), in the 1990s found themselves in effect separated in many instances from men with whom heretofore they had joined forces in resistance. Though work in the field continues to be done with kinship groupings, the "communal form of power" under the sign of the cultural nationalist family may be bankrupt, especially for female wage-workers. Of course, the attempt to bring men and women together under conservative notions of the "family" may be a misnaming in lieu of a search for a more apt term for communitarian solidarity.

Whether as domestic servants, canners, or in the service industry in the United States, or as electronic assemblers along the U.S./ Mexican border, these "new" women-subjects find themselves bombarded and subjected to multiple cross-cultural and contradictory ideologies—a maze of discourses through which the "I" as racial and gendered self is hard put to emerge and runs the risk of being thought of as "irrational" or "deluded"—in their attempt to articulate their oppression and exploitation. In the face of Anglo-European literacy and capitalist industrialization, which interpellates them as individuals for example, and the "communal mode of power" (as mode of defeudalization; Spivak 1988: 224), which interpellates them as "Mothers" (the bedrock of the "ideal family" at the center of the nation-making process, despite discontinuous modes of its construction), the figure and referent of the Chicana today is positioned as conflictively as Lyotard's "differend." She is the descendant of the Native women who are continuously transformed into mestizas, Mexicans, émigrés to Anglo-America, Chicanas, Latinas, Hispanics—there are as many names as there are namers.

Lyotard defines differend as "a case of conflict, between (at least) two parties, that cannot be equitably resolved for lack of a rule of judgment applicable to both arguments. One side's legitimacy does not imply the other's lack of legitimacy" (1988: 11). In appropriating the concept as a metonym for both the figure and the referent of the Chicana, for example, it is more important to note that though it enables us to locate and articulate sites of ideological and discursive conflict, it cannot inform the actual Chicana differend engaged in a living struggle to seize her "I" or even her feminist "We," to change her circumstances without bringing into play the axes in which she finds herself in the present—culturally, politically, and economically.

The call for elaborated theories based on the "flesh-and-blood" experiences of women of color in *This Bridge Called My Back* (Moraga and Anzaldúa 1981) may mean that the Chicana feminism project must interweave the following critiques and critical operations:

1. Multiple cross-cultural analyses of the ideological constructions of raced Chicana subjects must be made in relation to

the differently positioned cultural constructions of all men and some Anglo-European women.

2. There must be a negotiation for strategic political transitions from cultural constructions and contestations to "social science" studies of referentially grounded Chicanas in the political economy.

3. These cultural constructions and contestations must critically examine the experiences of Chicanas who live out their experiences in heterogeneous social and geographic positions.

Though not all women of Mexican/Hispanic descent would call themselves Chicanas, I would argue that it is an important point of departure for critiques and critical operations (on the jointure/ bridge) that keep the excluded within any theory-making project. That is, in the Mexican-descent continuum of meanings, Chicana is still the name that brings into focus the interrelatedness of a class/ race/gender and forges the link to actual subaltern Native women in the U.S./Mexico dyad. In negotiating points 1 and 2, how can we work with literary, testimonial, and pertinent ethnographic materials to enable Chicanas to grasp their "I" and "We" in order to make effective political interventions? This implies that we must select, in dialogue with women, from the range of cultural productions, those materials that actually enable the emergence of I/We subjectivities (Castellano 1990).

Given the extensive ideological sedimentation of the (silent) Good Woman and the (speech-producing) Bad Woman that enabled the formations of the cultural nationalistic "communal modes of power," Chicana feminists have an enormous mandate to make "sense" of it all, as Anzaldúa desires. It requires no less than the deconstruction of paternalistic "communal modes of power," which is politically perilous because often they appear to be the "only" model of empowerment that the oppressed have, though they have ceased to function for many women as development and postindustrial social research indicates. Also, it requires the thematization and construction of new models of political agency for women of color, who are always already positioned cross-culturally and within contradictory discourses. As we consider the diffusion of mass media archetypes and stereotypes of all women that continuously interpellates them into the patriarchal order according to their class, race (ethnicity), and gender, the "mandate" is (cross-culturally) daunting. Yet, "agent provocateurs" know that mass media and popular cultural production are always open to contestations and recodifications that can become sites of resistance (Castellano 1990).

Thus, the feminist, Chicana, activist, writer, scholar, and intellectual on the one hand has to locate the point of theoretical and political consensus with other feminists (and "feminist" men), and on the other continue with projects that position her in paradoxical binds: for example, breaking out of ideological boundaries that subject her in culturally specific ways, and crossing over to cultural and political arenas that subject her as "individual/autonomous/neutralized" laborer. Moreover, to reconstruct differently the raced and gendered "I's" and "We's" also calls for a rearticulation of the "You's" and "They's." Traversing the processes may well enable us to locate points of differences and identities in the present to forge the needed solidarities against repression and oppression, or, as Lorde (1984) and Spivak (1988) would have it, locate the "identity-in-difference" of cultural and political struggle.

Note

I would like to thank the late Gloria Anzaldúa, Rosa Linda Fregoso, Francine Masiello, and Margarita Melville for their reading and comments on this essay. Responsibility for the final version is, of course, mine.

References

Acuña, Rodolofo. *Occupied America: A History of Chicanos.* New York: Harper & Row, 1981. Published in 1972 as *Occupied America: The Chicano's Struggle Toward Liberation.* San Francisco: Canfield Press.

Alarcón, Norma. "Traddutora, Traditora: A Paradigmatic Figure of Chicana Feminism." *Cultural Critique* 13 (Fall 1989): 57–87.

———. "The Theoretical Subject(s) in *This Bridge Called My Back* and Anglo American Feminism." In *Making Face, Making Soul/Haciendo Caras*, edited by Gloria Anzaldúa, 356–369. San Francisco: Spinsters/Aunt Lute, 1990.

Allen, Paula Gunn. "Who is Your Mother? Red Roots of White Feminism." In *Multicultural Literacy: Graywolf Annual Five*, edited by Rick Simonson and Scott Walker, 13–27. St. Paul, MN: Gray Wolf Press, 1988.

Anzaldúa, Gloria. *Borderlands La Frontera: The New Mestiza*. San Francisco: Spinsters/Aunt Lute, 1987.

Barrera, Mario, et al. "The Barrio as Internal Colony." In *People and Politics in Urban Society*, edited by Harlan Hahn, 465–498. Los Angeles: Sage, 1972.

Castellano, Olivia. "Canto, locura, y poesía: The Teacher as Agent-Provocateur." *The Women's Review of Books* 8, no. 5 (1990): 18–20.

Cordova, Teresa, et al., eds. *Chicana Voices: Intersections of Class, Race, and Gender*. Austin, TX: Center for Mexican American Studies, 1986.

Giménez, Martha. "The Political Construction of the Hispanic." In *Estudios Chicanos and the Politics of Community*, edited by Mary Romero and Cordelia Candelaria, 66–85. Boulder, CO: National Association for Chicano Studies, 1989.

Hurtado, Aida. "Relating to Privilege: Seduction and Rejection in the Subordination of White Women and Women of Color." *SIGNS* 14, no. 4 (1989): 833–855.

Kauffman, Linda. "The Anti-Politics of Identity." *Socialist Review* 1 (1990): 67–80.

Lorde, Audre. *Sister Outsider: Essays and Speeches*. Trumansburg, NY: Crossing Press, 1984.

Lyotard, Jean-Francois. *The Differend: Phrases in Dispute*. Translated by Georges Van den Abbeele. Minneapolis: University of Minnesota Press, 1988.

McLaughlin, Melton. *Celia, A Slave*. New York: Avon Books, 1991.

Melville, Margartia, ed. *Twice a Minority: Mexican American Women*. St. Louis, MO: C. V. Mosby, 1980.

Mies, Maria, et al. *Women: The Last Colony*. London: Zed, 1989.

Molyneux, Maxine. "Mobilization without Emancipation: Women's Interests, the State, and Revolution in Nicaragua." *Feminist Studies* 2, no. 2 (1985): 227–254.

Mora, Magdalenda, and Adelaine R. del Castillo, eds. *Mexican Women in the United States: Struggles Past and Present*. Los Angeles: Chicano Studies Research Center, University of California, 1980.

Moraga, Cherríe, and Gloria Anzaldúa, eds. *This Bridge Called My Back: Writings by Radical Women of Color*. Watertown, MA: Persephone Press, 1981.

Munoz, Carlos, Jr. *Youth, Identity, and Power: The Chicano Movement*. London: Verso, 1989.

Rojas, Guillermo. "Social Amnesia and Epistemology in Chicano Studies." In *Estudios Chicanos and the Politics of Community*, edited by Mary Romero and Cordelia Candelaria, 54–65. Boulder, CO: National Association for Chicano Studies, 1989.

Ruiz, Vicki L., and Susan Tiano, eds. *Women on the US-Mexican Border: Responses to Change*. Winchester, MA: Allen & Unwin, 1987.

Spivak, Gayatri Chakravorty. "Can the Subaltern Speak?" In *Marxism and the Interpretation of Culture*, edited by Cary Nelson and Lawrence Grossberg, 271–313. Chicago: University of Illinois, 1988.

Trinh, Minh-ha T. *Woman/Native/Other*. Bloomington: Indiana University Press, 1989.

Warren, Scott. *The Emergence of Dialectical Theory: Philosophy and Political Inquiry*. Chicago: University of Chicago Press, 1984.

Zavella, Patricia. *Women's Work and Chicano Families: Cannery Workers of the Santa Clara Valley*. Ithaca, NY: Cornell University Press, 1987.

10

Chapped with Weather and Age: Mixed-Blood Identity and the Shape of History

Sara C. Sutler-Cohen

I imagine her house a shambled two-story shack, perhaps set back from the street a bit, and beset with rusted tin cans and chipped marbles, with their once-bright promise of an earthen tint faded now to brown mud. Maybe the house also tilts a bit to the left, sinking slowly into the southern soil. I can picture her—perpetual bandages on her knees, one dingy sock pulled higher than the other, and a hand-me-down dress stained with blackberries or ketchup, eclipsing the flowered pattern. She would have her bits of sticky brown-black hair tied back with a thin white cloth while sitting on the back steps waiting for her Grampa Otis to spread his gigantic arms around her as he sat and talked to her about history and maybe some stunted politics. In my mind, it is quiet there, but that's probably not the case. I like to think of her home as serene, and not raging; I know enough of the truth of it, however, to feel even from here, nearly sixty years distant, the walls buckle with the scent of my Grampa Joe, my mom's dad, swollen from drunken rage and hatred as he chased his father away every time he came to see my mom.

My memory is full of bits and scraps of someone else's history; not unlike an interesting series of short stories, perhaps by Harper Lee (I often imagined my mom as a half-Indian Scout and my grampa a sober Cherokee Atticus), but rarely did I fantasize that this was at all part of my bloodline. My mom used to tell me stories about my great-grandpa, Grampa Otis. She remembers him a giant in her child's eye. His hair had gone white and swung loosely below his waist. He sometimes wore it free, but once in awhile he would bind it with a braid. Sausaged fingers stained ocher with nicotine at the creases and joints, chapped with weather and age. He wore a dark ginger hue to his skin, and his eyes, Mom would say, were so brown as to be black, and soft around the edges. He had a husky voice from years of sin, and they would sit together and talk or just look up into the night sky, counting stars on a clear night in Baltimore. Or D.C. Or somewhere in West Virginia. It may have actually been North Carolina. I'm not entirely sure, as homespace has been a muddled memory for my mother.

The landscape of what the Sutlers called home changed with my grandfather's gambling and drinking habits. Before he settled as a famous-in-his-neighborhood butcher, Grampa Joe would traipse up and down the states, settling where he wasn't being looked for. By the time my uncles and aunt came along, they were pretty much settled in West Virginia and the visits from Grampa Otis were but a memory. As she is considerably older than my uncles and my aunt, my mother was the only one visited by him. Grandmother Helen was a British adoptee and a staunch Southern Baptist Methodist; any talk of being Indian was beat out of the family. This may be the sole reason my mom received the metal end of the belt and the boys only the fleshy leather. I'm not sure she ever got over the ceased visits.

My great-great-grandfather took the name Sutler during the Civil War because that's what he did for a living. By definition, a sutler is a civilian who sets up shop to sell provisions to soldiers. In my great-great-grandfather's case, he did this for the Confederates. So it's likely that if you know anyone with the surname of Sutler, bets on that's my kin. In California, there's me, my mom, and my uncle Butch, whom I met when I was eight at my grandmother's funeral in D.C., and who lives somewhere in Southern California with his wife and doesn't know he's got not only Irish and English blood running through his veins, but that the rest is Cherokee. The rest of the Sutler clan is in the Southeast, and my mom is violently estranged from them. Grampa Joe died some years back, and my mother and Aunt Linda hate each other. My uncle Rick was stabbed to death in a bar brawl he tried to break up, and my uncle Ray died from lung cancer, like my Grampa Joe who chain-smoked nonfiltered Camels, wheezing his collapsing lungs into a coma of their own.

When my great-great-grampa changed his name to Sutler he really was a sutler during the war, and the stories are not surprisingly, yet believably choppy as our family history is peppered with violent spasms, alcoholism, and ethnic denial. As was the case for so many people, as I understand it, if you could pass as white, you did. My great-grampa struggled with a disconnected relationship with his father, the original (S)utler, and eventually relocated over to Oklahoma where he met an Irish immigrant whose name has gone the way of so many memory slips, and there was born my Grampa Joe. Like his father, Grampa Joe also had a precarious relationship with his father and left Oklahoma, succeeding at suppressing his "Indianness" and leading a semi-white life with his new Brit-adoptee wife and having a gaggle of kids.

Many years later, I find myself trying to write it all down for an article on contestation and mixed-race identity. I'm not entirely sure why it matters, actually. There are times when I feel like I can just blend in with society as is. I don't look too Anglo, but by no means do I look too indigenous, and I'm a difficult pass for a Jew, the bloodlines I get from my father's side. But I am all of these things. I am all of this and none of this and therein lies the contestation. I've always been one of those people asked to answer the question "What are you, anyway?"

This contestation belies truth in a myriad of ways, not the least of which is the notion that being in touch with one's ethnic roots is freeing. I don't think too many people would argue with the idea that to be Indian today is in vogue. One look at the 2000 census tells us this—unless we venture to think that all of a sudden Native People are populating at an astounding rate in California, home to arguably the most diverse tribal peoples as well as teeming with "wanna-bes" and "plastic shamans." I'm not entirely convinced of the former—and do agree that indeed it may be in fashion to have a grandmother who was an Indian princess somewhere down the line. However, at least in some urban centers, it may not be so bad to be indigenous either—for those who indeed are. My point is that the self is contested within the confines of mixed-raced or mixed-blood identity because the notion of truth is inherently connected to

the imagination, and the imagination, bound up as it is with interpretation, ghosts, and dream states, is always shifting.

Being mixed race is complex and runs deeply into the ruins of
the mind. It is so often a diasporic identity—and the idea of emotional homelessness is not far off that road. We live in a society of
spectacle; in an eternal Goffman-esque landscape in a world based
on the visible. Mixed-raced outcasts are seemingly rooted in exile
from all sides. One may not be all (Jewish, Irish, British, Cherokee/
Tsalagi, for instance) because these ethnic enclaves need often to be
one. It's sometimes easier, in other words, to be just Jewish (or Irish
or English or Cherokee) and not face up to other lines of ancestry.
It's seen as a foible to lay claim to all and not one. Contrarily, one
may not be one either. For if you are only partially something, and
you claim it, are you then impinging on those who are completely
that something?

A point should be raised here. It's important, in thinking about
wrestling with the idea of contestation and identity, that the understanding of home be discussed. Some folks may argue that home
is not always the physical—that the idea of home is rooted in the
memory and a connection to the land, but perhaps the land is not
always tangible. For those of us who are descendants of Native
ancestry, home is itself a difficult, internal, emotional debate. Inside
this idea of home may also be a reframing of intellectual understand-
ings, with respect to where and who the Subject may be, particularly
when the Subject is neither and both.

How, for instance, does one become a Subject (whatever the
context/s) in a society, or in a community within a society, and subsequently in history? Is the Subject-as-self a site of semiotic embodiment
that is created by materialist affectations? And with that submission
(or willingness to embody materialism through the lens of, say, popular culture), how is the Subject realized as a category within the
definition/s of inequality and identity? In thinking this through, I
am drawn to forces within, from which memory is created and the
Subject is continually revised to help circumnavigate the hegemony
of the time—via performance. Ergo, to perform mixed-raced identity
is a relative impossibility. One first must agree that there are lines to
be drawn and acted upon (can you be all of these things?).

But to create and maintain a mixed-race identity may also be
a relative impossibility because the lines drawn in the sand often

morph into solid rock-walls. During my time as an undergraduate at an all-women's college, there rose a club for mixed-race students. But it was not trustworthy. We sat together, but not close. We suspected one another, looked each other up and down, desperately trying to figure out what we might all be. Every week we were to bring a dish and a discussion representative of some side or angle or corner or edge of some race or ethnicity we carried in our body politic. It always felt naked and violent. The spasms came from within, and no one spoke or made eye contact. I came with rushing heartbeats and clammy hands until I could no longer bear it. Everyone wanted a space to be comfortable, but nobody wanted to talk about being. It was just too difficult. Nobody could agree on being all—because being one, for the most part, was easier.

The idea of belonging and not belonging first struck me in that contested space where I felt as though for the first time my racial identity was suddenly punctuated by the eight or ten sets of eyes on me those days. Certainly we were all there because of that feeling of needing to belong. But it felt as though the need was greater to be not-White than it was to be of-color. In so many ways of course it's easier to pass as white and go unquestioned. There's really no challenge there. You shop, you eat, you parent, you go to school pretty much unruffled and unnoticed. Nobody looks at you askance; nobody asks what you are or if you speak English. You're shrouded in pleasant secrecy when you're mixed but look white because you have a hidden secret that enables you to walk in two worlds, but the second world, the buried one, is the one you have to scream out of to get noticed.

In the art of being mixed raced or mixed blood, one's identification in the world dictates one's privilege or lack thereof. When I was growing up, I was dark skinned. In the summers I stood out with thick black hair and dark olive skin that grew darker under the hot August sun. It blazed down on me unapologetically, and I felt impossibly ugly and vulnerable next to my mom, who wound up pale and green-eyed. If she was the Indian in my family, you could have fooled me. I always thought it was simply a cruel joke to make an excuse for the way I looked. But over sticky peanut butter and bacon sandwiches she would sit me down and tell me whispers of her past. How her grandfather would sneak around to see her and how her father, my Grampa Joe, resented the fact that he was an Indian and worked his entire life to erase who he was. Much later in life, in my twenties, I spent time brooding over some unnamed loss of who I was supposed to be. My brothers had long since left the family emotionally, and my mother had long since left me through mental illness. I was angry that I had no one to answer my one million questions and even more so that I felt like the only one that cared about our past. I flipped through AIM leaflets looking for some sort of struggle I could identify with but grew bored through my own ignorance and paced through life worrying about academic papers and rearing a child of my own.

Our stories set the landscape for mixed-race identity. It's the gut-wrenching realities that get underneath these questions of being mixed raced. My story is not so different than many other mixed-blood kids, be they part Laotian, Salvadoran, Tlingit, or if they can trace their trees to Erik the Viking. The question to consider is the one that asks who am I and who would I like to be. Because like it or not, those of us who can pass and do pass and live much freer lives as white people have it easy. We have the freedom to decide when and how much we want to be that other half or quarter or sixteenth or sixty-fourth. This becomes not surprisingly politically charged when someone else who walks the sidewalk wearing their race on their skin bumps into you and you don't know how to look back at them. And toeing that "I am Indian"/"I am not Indian" line that is too often drawn in a fog only makes it more complicated. Why should I care?

While I don't have a clear answer to this, and perhaps never will, it at least behooves us to think on the connection between the imagination and the sense of self that being mixed blood raises. It's likely that my life experiences have led me to my area of interest as a graduate student. In my dissertation I look at the growing field of contemporary shamanism, or neoshamanism, and focus in on the religious and racial positionality of people in what's called the shamanic community. The common trope is one that repeats, "I was an Indian in a previous life." It is at this highly politicized and hotly contested moment of claiming spiritual and personal homespace that the notion of being white *and* fill-in-the-blank-tribe begs to be unpacked. In interviewing and casually chatting with folks both pedestrian and infamous in shamanic circles, the passion sprouting from those few precious words of attachment to the "other" resonated deeply with each person who laid claim to their right to practice (and buy and sell) shamanism. In a word, Indian-ness is suddenly *felt*. But one could also posit that for these folks (all of them seemingly, if not admittedly, white) *feeling* Indian is a choice and not a matter of walking the somewhat literal Red Road. One could also suggest that this is fallout of vogue Indian-ness.

In northern California laying claim to being at all Native can line your pockets pretty thick and being mixed blood but looking white can cast suspicion and even distrust. So whoever said the personal is political was right—and it works both ways. The human condition, bound up with all of its complicated nuances, nearly always comes down to identity, and somehow if you can be in a position of wealth and power in this country and cross-pollinate your privilege with marginality, this is a recipe for success. So it should come as no surprise that I tend to be a bit reluctant to be seen as white and identify as a mixed blood, and writing out my stories and the stories of my families is terrifying, not because of our own muddled and violent history, but because I'm still trying to figure out how I came to be this mixed-up bundle of racial identities in the first place.

I'm beginning to apologize for who I am now, and that would be defeatist—something I like to refuse to be. My Indian friends insist on my fleshing out that part of me that is indigenous, but I can't help feeling like a fraud for it, or feeling like I'm ignoring my great-grandma Sara, a fervid nonpracticing Jewish anarchist, who ran women's meetings while sucking on a stogie and never cracked a smile in all the pictures I have of her. Or my grandfather, Sara's son Max, who put up with racial slurs and backhanded slaps during World War II when he fixed the teeth of Southern soldiers during the war. If I insist on being only Cherokee, am I left with a void, a dark tunnel with my relatives beckoning me to remember them? If I insist on being Cherokee, I am left scrambling because even on a good day, I don't know much. If I insist on being Cherokee, does it mean I cross the line from descendant into an unknown realm of ancestry? Can I even claim that? We're not on any rolls I ever heard of, and I know everyone with the surname of Sutler is my relative and will likely only identify as white.

So there is more to this than just what people think I should claim. Some of my Native friends beckon me to press on as an Indian scholar. Some don't really care. Some of my white friends e-mail me calls for papers requesting Indian scholars, and I shy away from that because I don't feel I can honestly claim that. Someone once said to me that there is a huge difference between being a descendant and being Native from a Native community, and it's this line I teeter on. The familial erasures and fusion of histories have clashed violently with federal policy about what it means to be an Indian, and who can decide if you are an Indian, so this coupled with my own existence makes for a confusing inner battle.

In the end, I can only write about what I know. I can argue with myself all day about who I am and how I came to be, but for those of us struggling with questions of identity, we only have our stories to hang on to. I have no enrollment number, no card verifying in writing that the blood running through me is indigenous and Irish and Russian/Polish and possibly either English or Romany. I do have stories and memories, and my ancestors know who I am, even if I don't. Mixed-blood peoples are every bit of who they are, and to deny our rights to ponder, to worry, and to think on these things is to deny ourselves full human potential. The uncertainties are endless, but to give up on those remaining questions is not a solution to understanding ourselves and the contestations of identity construction. The debate remains at the forefront of not only Native American and Indigenous studies, but in life itself. We are the shapers of history.

Note

I want to acknowledge that I am not writing here as a member of a federally recognized tribe. There is a distinction between having Indian ancestry and growing up in a sovereign tribal community. It is with this in mind that I write as a mixed-blood person of Indian descent who grew up in an urban area. There are many people of mixed Native ancestry who respect and acknowledge their Indian heritage, and it is with sincerity that I write from this particular experience and perspective.

11

Playing Indian

Carolyn Dunn

> Out of her body she pushed silver thread, light, air
> and carried it carefully on the dark, flying
> where nothing moved.
> Out of her body she extruded
> shining wire, life, and wove the light
> on the void.
> From beyond time,
> beyond oak trees and bright clear water flow,
> she was given the work of weaving the strands
> of her body, her pain, her vision
> into creation, and the gift of having created,
> to disappear.
> After her, the women and the men weave blankets
> into tales of life, memories of light and ladders,
> infinity eyes, and rain.
> After her I sit on my laddered rain-bearing rug
> and mend the tear with string.
>
> —Paula Gunn Allen, "Grandmother,"
> *Life Is a Fatal Disease: Collected Poems*

The Laguna Pueblo/Sioux/Lebanese/Scottish poet, novelist, and scholar Paula Gunn Allen related a story once of how, at an MLA conference a few years ago, a colleague asked the question, "Is there such a thing as American Indian literature?" to which Allen looked around the room and answered, chuckling, "Yes."[1] In spite of the successes of several novels written by American Indian writers over the last thirty years, there still has been a reluctance on the part of literary scholars to acknowledge the existence of an American Indian literature or literary tradition. From Hum Ishu Ma's (Mourning Dove, or Cristal Quintasket Galler) *Cogewa the Halfblood* (published in 1927) to D'Arcy McNickle's *The Surrounded* (published in 1936), American Indian oral traditions were passed down generation to generation by storytellers, becoming what is today known as the American Indian literary tradition, stories that incorporate ceremony and myth and legend with traditional Anglo/Euro American story elements.[2] These early storytellers wove elements of Western literary traditions with tribal or collective concerns based within their tribal groups. In spite of this blending of traditional Western story elements with Native American traditions, *Cogewa the Halfblood* is not a typically Western story. Like many novels by Native American writers, *Cogewa* incorporates the clash and effect of two cultures: Western melodrama (the popular literature style of the time) appearing alongside with Okanogan tribal history, politics, worldview, and spirit essences, or, as Allen refers to it in *The Sacred Hoop*, "spirit based understanding."[3]

McNickle follows along the literary style that Mourning Dove used in her marriage of Indian and Western literacisms: assimilation. Archile Leon is McNickle's half-breed protagonist, caught in the conflicting worldviews of the American and Native American worlds. McNickle, like Mourning Dove, uses tribal ritual and Salishan tradition to illuminate his novel, but his novel suggests that Native American survival hinges upon assimilation: the only way Native Americans are to survive is to completely adapt to the ways of the Western world.

Besides Mourning Dove and McNickle, little contemporary work of a noticeably Native literary tradition was published until N. Scott Momaday's Pulitzer Prize–winning *House Made of Dawn*, in 1969. *House Made of Dawn* is a novel that blends traditional Navajo tribal elements of storytelling and the importance of storytelling to the continuing ritual tradition and myth held by the tribes, and the relationship of the story to the tribal center as part of what is called tribal aesthetics.[4] Continuing in that tradition was James Welch with *Winter in the Blood* (1974) and *The Death of Jim Loney* (1979); Leslie Marmon Silko with *Ceremony* (1977), *Storyteller* (1981), and *Almanac of the Dead* (1991); Janet Campbell Hale's *The Jailing of Cecelia Capture* (1981); Louise Erdrich's award-winning novels of Chippewa life, *Love Medicine* (1984), *The Beet Queen* (1986), *Tracks* (1988), *The Bingo Palace* (1995), *The Antelope Wife* (1999), *The Last Report on the Miracles at Little No Horse* (2001), and *The Master Butcher's Singing Club* (2002); Paula Gunn Allen's novel *The Woman Who Owned the Shadows* (1983); Susan Power's *The Grass Dancer* (1995); Debra Earling's *Perma Red*; and Sherman Alexie's *Reservation Blues* (1996) and *Indian Killer* (1998)—all novels written by and about American Indians that have drawn attention to the Native literary tradition and model.

Since the publication of Momaday's *House Made of Dawn* in 1969, Indian novelists have transformed the oral traditions of their individual cultures into novels that express the multiplicitous nature of Indian life. A multiplicitous nature relates to the endurance of an existence of two very different worlds: the Indian world(s) and the Anglo/Euro American world of North America. Into this multiplicity Indian writers are weaving threads of traditional ceremonial myth and ritual into blankets that encompass two, if not more, ethnic and literary traditions. Besides a Western and Indian tribal influence, today's contemporary Indian writers can and do utilize other tribal traditions as well. Momaday, a Kiowa and Cherokee Indian, writes of the Navajo Blessingway ceremonies in *House Made of Dawn*, modeling the structure of the novel after the classic Navajo structure of the Chantway system; Turtle Mountain Chippewa Erdrich tell the story of protagonist Vivian Two Star's Navajo and Arapaho bloodlines. These dual bloodlines allow Indian writers to weave in threads of an almost pan-Indian tribalism, a coming together of all nations, a relationship of Native writer to non-Native ancestral landscape. Writers like James Welch, Gerald Vizenor, Paula Gunn Allen, Leslie Marmon Silko, and Louise Erdrich have begun to tell their stories of poverty, isolation, triumph, myth, love, ritual, resistance, regeneration, intertribal relations, ceremony, and survival in their novels, incorporating structural devices and tropes drawn from the oral traditions. The written word has become a contemporary Native tradition, stories being passed to and handed down to new generations via publication. Paula Gunn Allen in her *Grandmothers of the Light: A Medicine Woman's Sourcebook* and our coedited volume *Hozho: Walking In Beauty*, Joseph Bruchac in *American Indian Tales*, and Leslie Marmon Silko in *Storyteller* keep the storytelling traditions alive now in literary form. Survival is tradition passed down generation to generation. If the stories survive, then the people survive.

In *The Sacred Hoop*, Paula Gunn Allen writes that there are two basic forms of Indian literature: ceremony and myth. Ceremony is a ritual reenactment of a specialized perception of a cosmic relationship, while myth is a prose record of that relationship.[5] According to Allen the literary tradition within American Indian cultures forms an unbroken line in the oral tradition from "time immemorial to the vital now."[6] These stories, in their oral and written form, are instruments of resistance against Western (Anglo/European) occupation. These stories, many of which are part of ritual traditions—creation stories and myths—are a means of survival and recognition of self and community in the face of the Western stereotype of the "vanishing/ed race." In telling these stories, American Indian writers prove that all of us who are peoples of sovereign nations and societies are indeed still alive. Creation stories and myths[7] preserve tribal identity. Literature, in turn, preserves tribal identity in modern times.

Tribal Identity, Aesthetics, and Performance of Place

> A performative is the semiotic gesture that is being as well as doing. Or, more accurately, it is a doing that constitutes a being; an activity that describes what it creates.
>
> —J. L. Austin

The formation of tribal identity is problematic at best. Traditionally, tribal clan systems defined tribal membership and identity. When the U.S. government recognized American Indian tribes as sovereign yet dependent nations,[8] it entered into a trust relationship with Indian nations, reverberations of which are still felt in Indian country today. The U.S. government has insinuated itself in determining membership in American Indian tribes.[9] The notion of identity politics takes on another dimension when discussed within the context of American Indian identity and racial formation. According to Judith Butler, "The foundational reasoning of identity politics tends to assume an identity must first be in place in order for political interests to be elaborated and, subsequently, political action to be taken."[10]

The formation of "the" American Indian culture is a notion wholly formed by the "other" in this instance—the self being first of all the familial identification, second the clan identification, then tribal or national identification, all of which is defined by not only the individual Native self but the Native community of which the "self" is related to, and part of. "The" American Indian "culture" is a racial formative designated upon a group of individuals by "the other" outside of the particular tribal or ethnic identity; the "other" that is a colonizing power therefore has determined the racial formation and subjection of the Native "other" in this instance. The term "American Indian" is not what an Indian person tends to identify him or herself as; for example, within the Muskogee (Creek) Nation, one identifies oneself by clan affiliation, tribal affiliation, then Native ancestry; one rarely defines oneself as "American Indian" only. Muskogees have become defined and subjected as "American Indian" by the colonizing "other," à la Althusser's doctrine of interpellation.[11] The American Indian tribal and clan identity was formed long before colonization, and that identification formation still informs the identity of tribal and clan members today. The Native Hawaiian People have a long tradition of identification: When meeting others in a group setting, an individual relates, through song/chant, the ancestral formation of identity in the repetition of names and deeds of ancestors, identifying place of birth, ancestor's place of birth, and sense of relationship to the place of birth and to the landscape from which one is formed. The connection between the interrelationship of ancestral identity, through language, landscape, and genealogy, becomes imperative in the formation of identity of the Native Hawaiian without the racial formation or designation of "Native Hawaiian" as given in subjection by the colonizing power. The traditional Native Hawaiian and the traditional Muskogee therefore have a formation of identity that predates the formation of subjection by the colonizing power. Butler, in her discourse on subjection in *The Psychic Life of Power*, posits, "Power imposes itself upon us, and, weakened by its force, we come to internalize or accept its terms. What such an account fails to note, however, is that the 'we' who accept such terms are fundamentally dependent on those terms for our existence."[12]

Butler's argument is especially provocative in American Indian circles on many complex levels. I argue that racial formation of Native

Peoples whose ancestors are indigenous to the Americas is multi-layered and complex and cannot be defined only in its relationship to power and to the colonizing power. The colonizing power, the United States, has indeed contributed to Althusser's outside "call of identity" and subject formation in regard to America's Native Peoples. First is the traditional formation of identity I mentioned earlier that within Muskogee society, as well as Laguna Pueblo society, is based upon clan and familial identification, genealogical identification that posits itself outside of the theory of interpellation and subject/object formation by the colonizing/power hierarchical other. Both Muskogee and Laguna societies are matrilineal, matrifocal, traditionally gynocratic societies whose identity is formed within societal structures, rather than by an outside colonizing power. Native Hawaiian identity has also been formed long before current power structures were hammered into place; racial formation is once again based upon genealogy and ancestral landscape identification. However, placing traditional methods of identity formation and modern interpellation, following Butler and Althusser, has thereby formed the identity of the contemporary American Indian. Further complicating the formation of identity is the inter-marriage between tribes and nontribal members that have created the new "mixed-blood," "pan-Indian" tribal identity that has formed in urban areas in the United States far away from ancestral homelands, which played a role in identity formation. Consciousness, according to Butler, "makes subjects of us all";[13] however, tribal consciousness was formed long before the consciousness of colonization and the colonizing American power put the call out to indigenous peoples. The term of colonization, or the call, is the term "American Indian" or "Native American," the umbrella term that classifies multilingual, multicultural as a whole into a homogenous consciousness that before colonization was not recognized. However, tribal and clan identity was formed long before the call, and in acknowledging the call tribal identity performs consciousness and the call of subjection becomes the antecedent of American Indian identity for the modern indigenous American. Tribal and clan identity, therefore, precede the call to subject formation by the colonizing power, and thus the formation of tribal and clan identity is the call which ancestrally speaks the self into being.

The late Louis Owens, in his essay "Beads and Buckskin: Reading Authenticity in Native American Literature," posits his theory of mixed-blood identity in American Indian literature:

"For Native Americans, the term in 'Indian' is a deeply contested space, where authenticity must somehow be forged out of resistance to the authentic representation . . . since the simulated Native 'Indian' is a Euramerican invention."[14]

The modern "American Indian" forms his or her identity not just through interpellation but through centuries of ancestral identification, through landscape identification and the sense of place from which the tribal center has emerged. Power centers, through the colonizing power and through tribal power, further informs the sense of self and identity for the modern American Indian. Years of forced relocation and genocide contributed to the formation of American Indian racial identity.[15] Owens's thesis reveals forms of resistance through literature and art of American Indians, of tribal peoples, of clan members, of familial organizations. Writing (and art) is a mode of resistance to the American ideal of the "American Indian." Writing is an act of being an indigenous person, of being Muskogee, Cherokee, Laguna, Native Hawaiian, each tradition coming from the landscape and cultures of which one is born. The role of the storyteller, in its traditional form, puts forth the call to tribal and clan consciousness in which the subject turns and responds to from a place of tribal identity. Language is the call, but language that precedes current colonizing power structure and therefore forms identity prior to colonizing subject formation.

The result of colonization and government policies of termination and relocation have resulted in a substantially large, multitribal population of young indigenous peoples existing as second- and third-generation urban American Indians, with or without tribal relations "back home" intact. The role of the traditional and modern storyteller is the role that forms the subject ancestrally and represents "the call" from home. The late Lee Francis III wrote about his son Lee IV's experience as an urban Indian in the essay "We The People: Young American Indians Reclaiming Their Identity":[16]

My son was born in Fairfax, Virginia. He is an urban. Since infancy, my spouse and I told our son story. We told story about all of creation, seen and unseen. We told him about the People. We told

> him story about the People of Fairfax, Virginia. He learned about the civil war and the pogroms committed against the People. We told him stories that incorporated that values, attitudes and beliefs of the People. We told stories about hummingbird and coyote and the tree people and the cloud beings. . . . It is a sad reality that a majority of urban Native students do not have a clue about the trials, tribulations, joys, and hopes of the People.[17]

For many young urban American Indians, the concept of the landscape of home is a faraway image told of only in story from those who left it behind. Many young Indians have no concept of their tribal identity, and an outside "other" constructs that identity for them. The return home then becomes an important aspect to a ritual of remembrance for many young urban American Indians. The role of story takes on the role of call, of prior subject formation, of identity, and of the performative of modern tribal and clan identity.

In *Red on Red: Native American Literary Separatism*, Craig D. Womack asserts that the need to return home to illuminate the artistic contributions of mixed-blood artisans to the Native canon is imperative. The return home, Womack argues, is what illumines the work in critical studies of American Indian literature. Womack also argues that the mixed-blood urban Indian must stop apologizing for his/her mixed-blood Native status and embrace their heritage(s); critics must also look to the home country of the artist to discuss their work(s). The connection between literature and landscape forms a criticism of its own that Womack argues for in his own critical work:

> I will seek a literary criticism that emphasizes Native resistance movements against colonialism, confronts racism, discusses sovereignty, and native nationalism, seeks connections between literature and liberation struggles, and, finally, roots literature in land and culture.[18]

This relationship between landscape and literature is imperative to the critical study of American Indian literature and the cultural production of American Indians; it is especially relevant to second-, third-, and fourth-generation urban American Indians whose ancestry is tribally, and nontribally, mixed. As critics, we must look to the mountain, as Gregory Cajete posits,[19] and yet we must also look to the ancestral landscape of the adopted country in order to further illumine the artist's production. We must recognize the importance of ancestral landscape as well as the adopted landscape in American Indian performativity. We must look to the tribal aesthetic of the ancestral and adopted landscape to recognize what performing Indian, performing tribal, performing indigenousness, is all about. We must recognize the modern storyteller and the performative act of storytelling in identity formation that represents both the "call" and the "performance" of "American Indian" identity in poststructuralist and postmodern terms. The indigenous trickster archetype and that role the indigenous storyteller embodies as indigenous performance calls subject formation into being. The storyteller's performance as trickster figure in tribal and clan society is what "the call" to identity formation is.

Tribal Consciousness/Tribal Aesthetics

In his work *The Signifying Monkey: A Theory of African American Literary Criticism*, Henry Louis Gates has discussed the trickster character in African folklore, Esu Elegbara/Legba as the character at the crossroads between humanity and divinity. Gates's concern is developing a theory of tribal aesthetic that will allow a cultural inquiry into African American texts that does not recontextualize or dispossess them. In so doing Gates himself has not only invoked the Divine Linguist/Spirit Esu and invited Esu to step into academia as well, but Gates himself has taken on the Esu persona as trickster and critic at the crossroads, a force that mediates between the sacred and the secular. The Signifying Monkey, a character from the African American vernacular tradition, embodies what Gates calls the "language of signifyin(g)."[20] Signifyin(g) is like, Gates says,

> Thinking about the black concept of Signifyin(g) is a bit like stumbling unaware into a hall of mirrors: the sign itself appears to be doubled, at the very least, and (re)doubled upon ever closer examination. It is not the sign itself, however, which has been multiplied.[21]

Signifyin(g) is tied in with language; it is a comment upon society built into the African American vernacular, which further comments on the oppressive qualities of mainstream society. An example of signifyin(g) would be rap music today. The rapper comments on injustice and racism and poverty while enjoying much success in mainstream music.

As he further explores the relationship between literary criticism and the African American vernacular tradition, Gates, like Esu, becomes the translator of meaning between humans and the gods. In Gates Esu/Elegbara is offered as a central part of an African American tribal aesthetic that in its present expression is based on secular spiritualism, for Esu is that elusive trickster at the crossroads, where the secular world and the spiritual world meet. Gates is concerned, however, that his theory will bring an element of mysticism to African American literature that can marginalize the ritualistic quality of the work:

> I have tried to define a theory of African American criticism not to mystify black literature, or to obscure its several delightful modes of creating meaning, but to begin by suggesting how richly textured and layered that black literary artistry indeed is.[22]

Likewise, Native American literature is richly textured and layered, complete with ritual and mythic elements that make up its various layers to explore this aspect of secular spiritualism. To separate Native American ritualistic and mythic elements from the tribal literary tradition is to perform a division between the sacred and the secular, which in "performing Indian" is unknown. Gates sees Esu/Legba personified in the critic, and in so doing the critic becomes the legendary African tribal trickster, the one who, "The Fon call Legba 'the divine linguist', he who speaks all languages, he who interprets the alphabet of Mawu to man and to other gods."[23]

The critic then, according to Gates's model, becomes Esu; the critic is the divine linguist who illuminates the text for the others, divine and otherwise worldly. The critic moves between the realm of the Divine, of the gods (the text), and illuminates the text (or interprets) for the masses. It is here, in the world of spirit, that shifting borderland between what is sacred and what is secular and the lack of difference between, that the trickster meets both spirit and human. It is here, in American Indian literature and tradition, that we meet the most famous trickster of all, Coyote. And here, with Indian women, Coyote takes on a different—female—

persona. Indian women, as Coyotesse, take the language of colonization, rework the language, and return it to the tribal center where it becomes the language of survival. This further illustrates Gates's idea of signifying: by reworking the language, Coyotesse tricks by using English (with its masculine terms and all) to tell the stories that were originally in Native tongues. The colonizer has been defeated by *his* own hand. Stories are survival. Stories in English become the trick, signified.

As Kenneth Lincoln comments in *Indi'n Humor*, Indian women writers, "coyotesses," become trickster characters in their own work. Ours is a symbolic return to the mythological world, achieved by using our collective tribal consciousness. In *Tracks* and *Love Medicine*, Louise Erdrich embodies several archetypal figures especially meaningfully—clan names Pillager and Nanapush; Fleur Pillager's relationship with the water monster Windigo; historical aspects of Indian boarding schools and timber industry claims to Chippewa land. Similarly, Gunn Allen in *The Woman Who Owned the Shadows* invokes Iyetiku, Thinking Woman, and the Laguna creation stories: "In the beginning was Spider. She divided the world. She made it. Thus thinking, She made the world,"[24] and Leslie Marmon Silko is equally effective in the mythological return in *Ceremony* (invocation of Ts'its'tsi'nako—Thought Woman, Grandmother Spider, Old Spider Woman, Tayo's illness seen due to his separation from the community—land, male, and female ceremony). In the Yellow Woman story from *Spider Woman's Granddaughters*, Silko gives a modern retelling of the traditional Yellow Woman (Irriaku, Corn Maiden) stories of the Cochiti and Laguna Pueblo Yellow Woman/Evil Katsina stories.[25]

Following Womack, it is evident that if as critics of literature we are to fully understand the text then we must immerse ourselves in the culture from which the text derives. Following Jung it is plain that the culture is the text and the literary artifacts rising from it are subtexts. This understanding of tribal values and views, a cultural understanding, will enable us to illuminate the texts accurately in the case of Leslie Marmon Silko's and Paula Gunn Allen's Yellow Woman stories from *Spider Woman's Granddaughters*. Critics must study the aspects of Laguna Pueblo deities Ts'its'naku (Thought Woman, Spider Grandmother) and her twin daughters, Naotsete and Uretsete (sometimes called Its'city), that the works allude to and take their meaning from. Ts'its'naku, or Spider Woman, thought the earth, the sky, the galaxy, all that is into being, and, as she thinks, so we are. She sang the Divine Sisters, Nau'its'ity and Ic'sts'ity (or Naotsete and Uretsete, or other various spellings and pronunciation, depending upon the Keres tribal dialect and transcription being used) into being out of her medicine pouch or bundle, and they in turn from their bundles the firmament, the land, the seas, the people, the katsina, the gods, the plants, animals, minerals, language, writing, mathematics, architecture, the Pueblo social system and every other thing you can imagine in this our world.[26]

According to the Keres, a gynocratic society whose language and social systems are traditionally matrilineal, matrifocal, and matrilocal, the world was created by the Grandmother Spider whose twin daughters created what remained of the world. Grandmother Spider is a creator deity common in both Southeastern and Southwestern cosmology, she who weaves the very fabric and design of the world and all that is within it. In many Pueblo stories collected by the anthropologist Franz Boas in the book *Keresan Texts*,[27] the stories of creation changed over the years, most likely due to the influence of Christianity on the tribes. Uretsete is presently seen as a male deity, the father who created the world, and Naotsete, his consort, as the mother:

A long time ago there in the north at the place of emergence below there our mother, corn-mother worked miracles. Everything that has names developed, the sun and the moon, and the stars and rainstorms and spirits and katsina and the shamans and game and the people were completed, then our mother Nau'ts'it'i [*sic*] *and our father I'tc'ts'it'i* said "how is it?" and our mother Nau'ts'it'i, "is it not yet done? Shall we not put out our children?"[28] (italics in original)

The story on the previous page, as told to Boas by Ko'tie in 1919, reflects the type of mythical storytelling told two centuries after Catholicism came to the Pueblo. The female supernatural Uretsete was incorporated into Christian mythology as the Father-Creator, and her sister Naotsete became the Mother-Consort whose creative powers were reduced to that of the consort of the male Creator. Whereas in the original stories Uretsete as Mother sang from her bundles the world with her twin, Uretsete as Father was given the duties of creation:

> Then our father I'tc'ts'it'i spoke thus, "No." said He. "first I shall divide the water and the land." Then spoke our Mother Na'ts'it'i, "Go ahead." Then our father said "let me try to see." Then to the mountaintop went our father I'tc'ts'it'i. Then there below he looked around. Then he divided the air and land. He shook it. There was shaking. Then he looked at it. Then he said, "Earth and water have become good." thus he said. Then he also said, "only the earth will be ripe," said I'cs'ts'it'i, our father. Then again the earth he turned inwards (toward himself). When he turned it there was a light breeze. Then next he turned the water and sky both.[29]

Evidence given in the version of *Emergence*, as told by Gi'mi (1919), talks of the distinction between the white father and the Laguna mother, showing that the Pueblo stories were influenced by Catholicism. Uretsete, seen within the passage, is still the father, but the storyteller specifically tells a story, distinguishing between the white people's father and the Laguna mother:

> There in the north long ago was the place of emergence and there also were our mother and our father. I'tc'ts'it'i, *this one was the white people's father. On her part this Nau'ts'it'i was short and this one was the Laguna people's mother.*[30] (emphasis added)

In her novel *The Woman Who Owned the Shadows*, Allen, performing Trickster, boldly asserts the archaic meaning behind the stories, that Grandmother Spider created the sacred twins and the twins were female:

> Within the pouches, the sacred identical pouches she had placed the seeds that would bear the woman who was her own twin. Uretsete and Naotsete she would name them, double woman she would name them, from whose baskets would come all that lives. In the Northwest she placed one, Placed one she in the northwest. . . . And they said, "We will name. We will think." Thus they said. Thus they sang. . . . Shaking, they were singing. Shaping the katsina and the spirits, the game and the mountains. Singing, chanting, shaking, crooning, they named everything. Thus they made everything ready for their children.[31]

In the prologue of her novel Allen performs Spider Woman her-self: giving back the power to the people, back through the blood-lines to the gynocratic society from which she was sung, back to the goddess/supernatural Spider Woman, back to Spider Woman's *daughters*, Naotsete and Uretsete. Here Allen becomes that Divine Linguist, that Esu/Trickster at the crossroads, the mediator between gods, giving the people back the power that the deities gave to begin with. She is performing Trickster, performing Laguna, performing clan, performing tribe. This is the role Trickster plays culturally, and this is the role the native woman, the woman of Laguna, inhabits and portrays to the inner and outer world.

These are powerful female supernaturals, these twins Naotsete and Uretsete, who in other aspects and other cultures have differ-ent names. To the Pueblo they are Uretsete and Naotsete; to the Dine (Navajo) they are Changing Woman and White Shell Woman; among the Quiche Maya they are Xmucane and Xepycoc, one of whom, Xepycoc, undergoes a similar sex transformation after Christianization. Among Erdrich's people, the Chippewa, the sis-ters Matchickkwewas and Oshkikwe retain their female identities, having Uncle Nanabozho (Nanapush) as the male aspect within the plot.[32] The multiplicitous nature of these deities can be overwhelm-ing. Educated in the Western monotheism, the Western scholar may be unable (or unwilling) to comprehend the multiplicity of the Pueblo, Dine, Maya, Chippewa, and Cherokee goddesses. For example, in one of her aspects, the great mother Uretsete is also known as Iyetiku, the mother of all Lagunas, the spiritual connec-tion between the mother/creator and the people.

Uretsete, as Iyetiku, establishes her connection to her children by giving the Pueblo the gift of corn. Corn is sacred to the Pueblo; in its seed aspect it is representative of the regeneration of the Pueblo people, and when it is eaten, it reaffirms the connection through physical sustenance of the goddess to the land and to the people who inhabit it. Iyetiku gave the people the Irriaku, the sacred ears of corn, as a gift to cement that connection, to bring it to a physi-cal reality. The Irriaku, or Yellow Women, (in one clan at least) are dressed in feathers to honor all things connected with Iyetiku: her creative powers, her gift to the people, the peoples' sacred connec-tion with the landscape. When the people honor the Irriaku, they honor themselves and the goddess that is the seed of tribal consciousness. The goddess is honored, the people are honored, the land is honored, all given physical manifestation in an ear of yellow corn.[33] To the Pueblo, the gifts of the goddess are seen in those yellow ears of corn, the Irriaku, and the connection between the divine mother/goddess and the children is substantiated. The spirit world becomes a physical reality in daily life through the Irriaku.

In her essay "Cuentos de la Tierra Encantado: Magic and Realism in the Southwest Borderlands,"[34] Allen explores the confluence of cultures (American Indian, specifically Navajo, Pueblo, Apache; Hispanic, and Euro-American) and landscape in the American Southwest.

> Besides food, stories provide a deep sense of continuity within a psychospace. A region is bounded and shaped by its climate and geography, but these features take on a human and spiritual dimension when rendered significant in narrative. The smells, sounds, and tactile sensations that go with a locale are as central to its human significance as the sights, and it is within the stories that all the dimensions of human sensation, perception, conception, and experience come together, providing a clear notion of where we are, who we are, and why.[35]

This confluence of cultures is what informs the interstices in these multiracial, multilingual spaces, and the study of place and space becomes important in looking at American Indian performance and the American Indian storyteller performing Trickster in story.

Womack posits in *Red on Red* that he disbelieves assimilation is a one-way process, that assimilation creates a culture that influences one another equally. The American Southwestern culture is a prime example of that process. Inclusive of cultures, the American Southwest has within its tenuous borders influences from Euro America, Native America, and Mexico. Two of the Southwest's most populated cities, Los Angeles and Denver, have the second- and third-largest populations of urban American Indians in the country. Tribal governments estimate that by the 2000 census, there were more Indians living in cities than there were on reservations or ancestral homelands. Certainly, these interacting cultures have a great influence upon one another, culturally, linguistically, mythologically, spiritually, even in the foods that are eaten. Stories tend to be told around tables, around food, around fires, around bars, around cultural centers, in theatres, in art. In performing Indian, writers, specifically Allen, are influenced by tribal center, Laguna culture, as well as the cultures that surround Laguna. And in this confluence, influences perceived and performed become culture bearer, as the Trickster herself. Performing Trickster is to perform culture, tribal culture, intertribal culture, and inform culture all around us.

Notes

1. Paula Gunn Allen, ed., *Studies in American Indian Literature* (New York: Modern Language Association, 1983).
2. Paula Gunn Allen, *The Sacred Hoop* (Boston: Beacon Press, 1986).
3. Allen, *The Sacred Hoop*, 83.
4. Paula Gunn Allen, *Spider Woman's Granddaughters* (Boston: Beacon Press, 1990).
5. Allen, *The Sacred Hoop*, introduction, xi.
6. Allen, *The Sacred Hoop*, 96.
7. The term *myth* has come to signify a falsehood in American language. When I use the term *myth*, I mean sacred stories and legends that have true meaning to a culture or a people, not necessarily a falsehood or a lie. The negative connotation tends to trivialize the myths—sacred stories and legends—of a people and reduce a culture, a way of thought or being, to something of nonimportance.
8. See the Marshall Trilogy of Supreme Court cases (*Cherokee Nation v. Georgia, Worcester v. Georgia, Johnson v. McIntosh*) in which the federal government, in a decision written by Chief Justice John Marshall, determined that Indian nations could cede land only to the federal government and not individuals and remaining Indian land would be held in trust for Indian nations with the federal government as the trustee for Indian nations, thereby making decisions for Indian nations based upon the trustor/trustee relationship, conferring upon Native nations the sovereign yet dependent status similar to a ward to his guardian.
9. An Indian may apply for membership in his or her tribe, but the federal government determines final say in membership, legally determining the blood quantum and identity of an Indian person in this country.
10. Judith Butler, *Gender Trouble* (New York: Routledge, 1999), 181.
11. Judith Butler, *The Psychic Life of Power* (Stanford, CA: Stanford University Press, 1997), 1.
12. Butler, *The Psychic Life of Power*, 2.
13. Butler, *The Psychic Life of Power*, 106.

14. Louis Owens, *Mixedblood Messages: Literature, Film, Family, Place* (Norman: University of Oklahoma Press, 1998).

15. The genocide perpetuated against American Indians by the United States is well documented. Ed and Bonnie Duran, in *Native American Postcolonial Psychology*, put it succinctly:

> For over five hundred years, Europeans have attempted to subjugate, exterminate, assimilate, and oppress Native American people. The effects of this subjugation and extermination have been devastating both physically and psychologically. Whole tribal groups have been devastated both physically and psychologically. . . . The policies of the U.S. government toward Native American people are shameful, particularly as they have been enacted by a government that preaches freedom and democracy. Even more shameful is the fact that this government has maintained a policy of termination of Native American people until recently. (28–29)

16. From MariJo Moore, ed., *Genocide of the Mind* (New York: Thunder's Mouth Press/Nation Books, 2003).

17. Moore, ed., *Genocide of the* Mind, 80–81.

18. Craig Womack, *Red on Red: Native American Literary Separatism* (Minneapolis: University of Minnesota Press, 1999), 11.

19. Gregory Cajete, *Look to the Mountain: An Ecology of Indigenous Education* (Durango, CO: Kivakí Press, 1993).

20. Henry L. Gates, Jr., *The Signifying Monkey* (New York: Oxford University Press, 1988).

21. Gates, *The Signifying Monkey*.

22. Gates, *The Signifying Monkey*.

23. Gates, *The Signifying Monkey*.

24. Paula Gunn Allen, *The Woman Who Owned the Shadows* (San Francisco: Spinsters, Ink, 1983), prologue.

25. Paula Gunn Allen and Leslie Marmon Silko are mixed-blood Natives from Laguna Pueblo in New Mexico. Traditional Laguna society, according to Allen, is matrilineal, matrifocal, and gynocratic, emphasizing the feminine as well as the masculine duality in society. Allen was born in Cubero, New Mexico, on a Spanish land grant near Laguna. Matrilineally Laguna as well as Scottish and Lakota, Allen is the middle daughter of a family of storytellers and poets. Her older sister, Carol Lee Sanchez, is a renowned poet; her late brother Lee Francis III was a poet and essayist as well. Allen's father, the late Lee Francis II, was the son of Lebanese cowboy immigrants to New Mexico and later served as lieutenant governor of the state. The storytelling influences in Allen's life are well documented; her generations of storytellers and poets have formed her identity as Laguna, Lebanese, Scottish, and Lakota. A poet and novelist as well as one of the foremost scholars

and critics of American Indian literature and American studies, Allen's creative work is not as well studied as her critical work is. Leslie Marmon Silko was born in Albuquerque in 1948, and is of mixed Laguna Mexican and Anglo ancestry. Growing up on the Laguna Pueblo reservation, she attended an Indian school and later attended school in Albuquerque and the University of New Mexico. Silko published her first short story, "Tony's Story," in 1969 and later wrote her first book of poetry, *Laguna Woman*, in 1974. Her first novel, *Ceremony*, was published in 1977, and is one of the most critically acclaimed novels by an American Indian novelist. Her "Yellow Woman" stories later appeared first in *Storyteller*, her 1981 collection of short stories and poems from Laguna. Although she is a most prolific poet and novelist, Silko, unlike New York and Los Angeles literary darlings Louise Erdrich and Sherman Alexie, is still primarily known as a Southwestern author and as, according to *Entertainment Weekly*, "the Native American novelist Leslie Marmon Silko." (In an article about novelist Larry McMurtry, Silko was the only one of McMurtry's girlfriends to be identified by a racial designation.) Both of these women are considered "founding mothers" of American Indian literature, yet their creative work has yet to stand alone as "literature" rather than "Native American literature," as, say, the work of an Erdrich or an Alexie has.

26. Franz Boaz, *Keresan Texts* (Washington, DC: Smithsonian Institution, 1932), 35–36.

27. Boaz, *Keresan Texts*.

28. Boaz, *Keresan Texts*, 39.

29. Boaz, *Keresan Texts*, 55.

30. Paula Gunn Allen, *Grandmothers of the Light* (Boston: Beacon Press, 1991).

31. Allen, *Grandmothers of the Light*.

32. Allen, *Grandmothers of the Light*.

33. Personal interview with Paula Gunn Allen, October 10, 1991, Seal Beach, California. Professor Allen detailed Laguna festival practices in relation to the Irriaku and the similarities between clan practices among the Pueblo tribes.

34. David M. Wrobel and Michael C. Steiner, eds., *Many Wests: Place, Culture, and Regional Identity* (Lawrence: University Press of Kansas, 1997), 342–346.

35. Wrobel and Steiner, eds., *Many Wests*.

References

Allen, Paula Gunn. *Grandmothers of the Light: A Medicine Woman's Sourcebook*. Boston: Beacon Press, 1991.

———. *Spider Woman's Granddaughters*. Boston: Beacon Press: 1990.

———. *The Sacred Hoop: The Recovery of the Feminine in American Indian Traditions*. Boston: Beacon Press, 1986.

———. *The Woman Who Owned the Shadows*. San Francisco: Spinsters, Ink, 1983.

———, ed. *Studies in American Indian Literature*. New York: Modern Language Association, 1983.

Boas, Franz. *Keresan Texts*. Washington, DC: American Ethnological Society, Smithsonian Institution, 1932.

Bouchard, Donald. *Language, Counter-memory, Practice: Selected Essays and Interviews by Michel Foucault*. Ithaca, NY: Cornell University Press, 1977.

Butler, Judith. *Gender Trouble: Feminism and the Subversion of Identity*. New York: Routledge, 1999.

———. *The Psychic Life of Power*. Stanford, CA: Stanford University Press: 1997.

Cajete, Gregory. *Look to the Mountain: An Ecology of Indigenous Education*. Durango, CO: Kivakí Press, 1994.

Capra, Fritjof. *The Turning Point: Science and Society and the Rising Culture*. New York: Bantam Books, 1982.

Duran, Eduardo, and Bonnie Guillory Duran. *Native American Postcolonial Psychology*. New York: State University Press of New York, 1995.

Ebron, Paulla. *Performing Africa*. Princeton, NJ: Princeton University Press, 2002.

Gates, Henry L., Jr. *The Signifying Monkey: A Theory of African American Literary Criticism*. New York: Oxford University Press, 1988.

Harjo, Joy. *How We Became Human: Poems 1975–2001*. New York: Norton, 2002.

Harjo, Joy, and Gloria Bird, eds. *Reinventing the Enemy's Language*. New York: W. W. Norton, 1997.

Jung, Carl Gustav. *Four Archetypes: Mother, Rebirth, Spirit, Trickster*. Princeton, NJ: Bollingen Series, 1968.

Kondo, Dorinne K. *About Face: Performing Race in Fashion and Theatre*. New York: Routledge, 1997.

Kristeva, Julia. *Revolution in Poetic Language*. New York: Columbia University Press, 1984.

Lewis, David, Jr., and Ann T. Jordan. *Creek Indian Medicine Ways: The Enduring Power of the Mvskoke Religion*. Albuquerque: University of New Mexico Press, 2002.

Lincoln, Kenneth. *Sing with the Heart of a Bear: Visions of Native and American Poetics*. Berkeley: University of California Press, 1998.

———. *Indi'n Humor*. London: Oxford University Press, 1993.

———. *Native American Renaissance*. Berkeley: University of California Press, 1983.

McNickle, D'Arcy. *The Surrounded*. Albuquerque: University of New Mexico Press, 1978.

Mihesuah, Devon A. *Indigenous American Women: Decolonization, Empowerment, Activism*. Lincoln: University of Nebraska Press, 2003.

Momaday, N. Scott. *House Made of Dawn*. New York: Perennial Library, 1988.

Moore, MariJo, ed. *Genocide of the Mind: New Native American Writing*. New York: Thunder's Mouth Press/Nation Books, 2003.

Mourning Dove. *Cogewa the Halfblood*. Lincoln: University of Nebraska Press, 1981.

Norwood, Vera, and Janis Monk, eds. *The Desert is No Lady*. New Haven, CT: Yale University Press, 1987. (Second edition: Tucson: University of Arizona Press, 1999.)

Ostriker, Alicia S. *Stealing the Language: The Emergence of Women's Poetry in America*. Boston: Beacon Press, 1986.

Owens, Louis. *Mixedblood Messages: Literature, Film, Family, Place*. Norman: University of Oklahoma Press, 1998.

Parker, Andrew, and Eve Kosofsky Sedgwick, eds. *Performativity and Performance*. New York: Routledge, 1995.

Sandoval, Chela. *Methodology of the Oppressed*. Minneapolis: University of Minnesota Press, 2000.

Schwaller de Lubicz, R. A. *Sacred Science*. English translation. Rochester, VT: Inner Traditions International, 1982.

Silko, Leslie Marmon. *Ceremony*. New York: Penguin Books, 1977.

Welch, James. *Winter in the Blood*. New York: Harper and Row, 1974.

Womack, Craig. *Red on Red: Native American Literary Separatism*. Minneapolis: University of Minnesota Press, 1999.

Wrobel, David M., and Michael C. Steiner. *Many Wests: Place, Culture, and Regional Identity*. Lawrence: University Press of Kansas, 1997.

12

Examining the Regional and Multigenerational Context of Creole and American Indian Identity

Andrew Jolivétte

> In articulation theory, the whole question of authenticity is set aside, and the process of social and cultural persistence is political all the way back. It's assumed that cultural forms will always be made, unmade, and remade. Communities can and must reconfigure themselves, drawing selectively on remembered pasts. The relevant question is whether, and how, they convince and coerce insiders and outsiders, often in power-charged, unequal situations, to accept the autonomy of a "we"? This to me is the more realistic way of talking about what is often termed cultural invention. . . . Struggles over anthropological and native authority have tended to obscure the historical challenge of representing sequential and overlapping processes of cultural continuity, rupture, transformation, and revival. I want to suggest that a lot of what has been referred to as invention can be rethought in terms of the politics of articulation.
>
> —James Clifford (2000)

I came to the question of Creole identity relatively early in life, but the implications have taken decades to unravel. In the early 1970s when my grandfather told my grandmother he didn't want "those niggas" (referring to my older half brothers whose biological father is African American) sitting next to "my grandchildren" (referring to my first cousins who are Creole and Puerto Rican), his actions were but the latest reflection of societal conflict played out on the familial stage. Fifteen years earlier, my father—along with my aunts, uncle, and paternal grandparents—had moved from southwest Louisiana to California. In the process, my grandparents informed him and the rest of the family that they were "becoming" a family of French Canadians, leaving their Creole identities behind. Why "French Canadians" as opposed to something else? This question, along with the rejection of blackness expressed in my grandfather's statement about "those niggas," continued to puzzle me across the years. It was not the privileging of whiteness that surprised me as much as the complexities of a racialization process that so thoroughly neglected the regionally and culturally specific identity of Creoles as a multigenerational mixed-race population. Our family situation speaks to the complex historical situation and sociocultural context in this country through which white is privileged over not only black but over mixed-race populations. Through the years, my interest in understanding this complex process led me back to Louisiana to document the contemporary cultural experiences and practices of Creole people.

In the late 1990s, I started to explore these issues from a different angle as I began collecting data on Creole-Indian relations. In the process, I discovered the Louisiana Creole Heritage Center (LCHC) at Northwestern State University in Natchitoches, Louisiana, and I attended the conferences they sponsored in Los Angeles, California, in July of 2001; in New Orleans, Louisiana, in October of 2003; and in Las Vegas, Nevada, in May of 2004, in which national attention was focused upon Creole studies and important questions were raised about the place of Indian, African, French, and Spanish contributions in the history, culture, and preservation of this multiracial community. Following the publication of Gary Mills's landmark work, *The Forgotten People*, in 1977, several key texts examined the history of Creoles of Color in the state of Louisiana, focusing particularly on the city of New Orleans and on the social, legal, and racial classification of Creoles as black or white, or black and white, but never as Indian (Dominguez 1997 [1987]; Woods 1989; Brasseaux, Fontenot, and Oubre 1996; Dormon 1996; Kein 2000).

In the United States and throughout the Americas, many communities of multiethnic, multicultural, and multiracial ancestry embody an aspect of American Indian identity that is seldom addressed publicly: the amalgamation of some indigenous tribes into new ethnic communities. The Creoles of southwest Louisiana are an example of one such community in which elements of the cultures of indigenous tribes have retained their vitality while intermingling with traditional Creole culture. By declaring many smaller Native communities in the Americas extinct due to disease, malnutrition, and European colonization, nineteenth- and twentieth-century scholars and researchers dismissed not just the contemporaneous contributions but also the continuing presence of indigenous groups such as the Atakapa and Opelousa descent Indians in southwest Louisiana, in effect erasing their existence by relegating it entirely to the past.

It is my contention, however, that groups such as the Opelousa and Atakapa not only still exist, but that they exist in new, complex, hybrid forms that thrive today within multiethnic and multicultural groups such as communities of Creoles of Color across the United States. In order to understand this phenomenon and to document the formation of ethnic and cultural identity among a complex multiethnic population, I embarked in 2001 upon an ethnographic study of Creoles of Color in North America, one of the few studies of Creole identity formation in the United States to explore contemporary Native identity among this population, and one of only a handful of studies which have drawn upon primary data collected from Creole people themselves. Those data, reported on in this article, contribute to our understanding of how racial identity and racial formation are articulated within a multigenerational, mixed-race Native population and provide a case study illustrating how other multiethnic populations throughout the Americas have blended with Indian groups to create a multiethnic American Indian diaspora.

Background

Despite a rich tradition of Creole studies in literature, media studies, and narratives of the antebellum South, little if any work in these disciplines has been devoted to examining the complex sociocultural relationship between Creole and American Indian identity. That is, few if any previous Creole studies link American Indian identity to the Creole American experience in the southern United States or to the growth of the Creole diaspora. Furthermore, most studies of Creole identity formation have been set in New Orleans, almost entirely overlooking the experience of Creoles in southwestern Louisiana. The three studies that examine the formation of a mixed-race French-Black Creole culture in New Orleans and thus offer a starting point for considering the social, political, and economic factors that have led to racializing Creoles in black and white terms—Mary Gehman's *The Free People of Color of New Orleans* (1994), Virginia Dominguez's *White By Definition: Social Classification in Creole Louisiana* (1997), and Gwendolyn Midlo Hall's *Africans in Colonial Louisiana: The Development of Afro-Creole Culture in the Eighteenth Century* (1992)—completely neglect to analyze the Indian experience within Creole culture during the eighteenth and nineteenth centuries.

No in-depth study to date of the U.S. policy of extermination through broken treaties, illegal land cession, and redefinition of Indian cultural and ethnic identity or community membership has looked specifically at mixed-race Indian identity in Louisiana. Similar lacunae characterize the research of scholars who have investigated the Creole experience of southwest and northwest Louisiana. Gary Mills's *The Forgotten People: Cane River's Creoles of Color* (1977) asserts that the Black Creole was originally accorded a third position (neither black nor white) within a three-tiered racial caste system but that this category has been collapsed over time to a black-only identity. Brasseaux, Fontenot, and Oubre's *Creoles of Color in the Bayou Country* (1996) focuses on areas of southwest Louisiana. Although these authors go a step further than their counterparts by at least partially addressing the Indian experience, their analyses leave many questions about what became of the Indians in southwestern Louisiana, some of which are illustrated in the following passage:

> Because indigenous inhabitants of the lower prairies—The Atakapas Indians—were reputedly cannibalistic, the Atakapas and Opelousas districts were among the last areas of lower Louisiana to be developed by the colony's French government. Indeed, the French administration made no effort to establish formal relations with the Atakapas, the area's largest Indigenous group, and the Opelousas, a cultural and linguistic subgroup of the Atakapas,

throughout the first four decades of Louisiana's existence, prompting the tribe to send a delegation to New Orleans in 1733 to forge commercial ties with the neighboring colony. (Brasseaux, Fontenot, and Oubre 1996: 6)

Here, Brasseaux, Fontenot, and Oubre raise the issue of the Atakapa presence in the area but provide no further mention or analysis of what becomes of this the "area's largest Indigenous group." The authors never explain what becomes of the Atakapa or the Opelousa tribes, nor do they acknowledge or discuss intermarriage or interracial sex between Indians and the French. The undisputable historical fact that there were few French women in the early settlements, however, means in effect that the first Creoles had to be of color and had to have Indian and/or African ancestry. Also problematic is the effect attributed by the authors to the Louisiana Purchase on tribal self-determination, land, and treaty rights (Deloria 1988). Since the Indians of the entire territory were uprooted, misplaced, and uncounted during this period, some scholars have inferred from the ensuing lack of records that all these Indians must have "died out," a position which I assert is unwarranted and historically inaccurate.

Instead, as Terrel Delphin, a Creole scholar from Natchitoches, Louisiana, explains, "Creoles understand Anglo-American racism, especially their conception of 'Negro blood,' as a powerful tool for disenfranchisement, leaving them unprotected and at distinct legal and social disadvantages" (1995: 14). He goes on to say,

Their Native American connections became confused in the Spanish period when, in the 1780s, Spain freed Indian slaves in Louisiana. Some were censused as Indians, others as freed slaves, still others as mulattos or mixed and some as blacks. Whenever Creoles tried to explain who they were, who they felt they were, it ultimately was, and is, interpreted as an attempt to *passer pour blanc*, an effort to deny an African connection. (1995: 14)

This assumption that Creoles *want* to pass for white continues to make identifying with their American Indian ancestry extremely difficult. The notion of "passing" is an important one in the face of ethnic resurgence theories which contend, however inaccurately, that many mixed-race people identify as Indian today for self-serving purposes, primarily economic and/or political. In fact, our ability to trace Indian-Creole relations with any accuracy has been clouded by the misdesignation of Indians as "colored" for most of Louisiana's history. Most interracial relationships in Louisiana were between European males and African or Indian females, who very often were the property of the men who seduced them. Research shows that most enslaved Indians were women, and that Indian women from the villages and female Indian slaves were "quickly absorbed into the Franco-African communities through concubinage and intermarriage" (Martin 2000: 59). Most of the slaves brought from Africa to Louisiana were male, whereas most Indian slaves were women who were sought primarily by French men to perform cooking, cleaning, farming, translating, and sexual duties. The large numbers of male African slaves and female Indian slaves inevitably meant that many slave families comprised African husbands and Indian wives. The slave communities on plantations and in cities like New Orleans developed as the respective Indian and African cultures evolved, melding into one common fabric. Children of African-Indian parentage were called "mulatto," while children of Indian females and French men were called "colored."

By the turn of the nineteenth century, the term "colored" was commonly used to describe people of either African or Indian heritage (Adams and Fusilier 2002). However, this aspect of Indian absorption into the Franco-African populations, yielding a hybrid and colonial Creole population, is mentioned only briefly if at all in most Creole studies, generally absent an analysis of how the Indian population, particularly the Native women, contributed to the continuity of the group's racial, ethnic, religious, and cultural identity. In fact, when Spanish governor Alejandro O'Reily outlawed Indian slavery in 1769, many slave owners simply reclassified the Indian slaves as black and thus kept them legally enslaved (Martin 2000: 59).

The study reported upon here builds on the work of Creole scholars like Delphin and Martin who have contributed to our understanding of historical aspects of the relations between Indians, Creoles, Africans, and Europeans, but places this history into a contemporary context. Additionally, I examine the failure of prominent anthropological and sociological theories in the twentieth century to document how American Indian individuals and groups, rather than falling into extinction as often claimed, were actually absorbed into multiethnic communities such as the Creole of Color communities in the state of Louisiana, where their living influence remains vibrant to this day.

Ethnic Identification and Self-Perceptions of Creoles in the United States

The present article examines ethnic self-identification of Creoles as well as factors associated with the misrepresentation of the group as biracial (black and white) rather than as multiracial (Indian, French, African, Spanish, etc.). This two-part ethnographic study deals first with quantitative data obtained through a national survey exploring Creole self-perceptions of identity as a multigenerational, mixed-race Indian population. The second set of data reported upon here was gathered through a series of structured and semistructured individual and group interviews about the politics of identifying as both Crèole and Indian.

Survey Design and Results

In order to explore the issue of how Creoles of Color have conceptualized, negotiated, and articulated their identities as members of a distinct multiracial community, I conducted a survey in August 2001 of one hundred randomly sampled members of a Creole Heritage Center mailing list that was made available to me through Northwestern State University in Louisiana. The survey included thirty-five questions, some open-ended and others closed. In a deliberate attempt to move beyond the limitations of the binary paradigm of identity in all questions related to racial, ethnic, and cultural identity, participants were invited to check as many answers as applied or to provide as many details as they felt appropriate.

The survey was distributed nationally to one hundred individuals who were members or otherwise affiliated with St. Augustine's Historical Society and the Louisiana Creole Heritage Center. Included in the mailing was a cover letter briefly describing the proposed plan for my dissertation research at the University of California, Santa Cruz, and requesting the recipients' participation.

Of these one hundred surveys, sixty were returned within a two-month period via the self-addressed, stamped envelopes that had been provided in order to protect participant anonymity, yielding an overall response rate of 60 percent. Participation in the study was strictly voluntary, with no remuneration or other financial incentives offered for participating.

The average age of the survey respondents was fifty-two years. More than 50 percent of the sample group worked as white-collar professionals. Fifty-three percent of the respondents were male, and 47 percent were female. Ten U.S. states (California, Illinois, Connecticut, Louisiana, Maryland, Mississippi, Missouri, New York, Tennessee, and Texas) and more than forty cities are represented by the sample group.

Despite the small size of the sample, the data collected clearly document a pervasive pattern of multiple self-identifications among Creoles that is inclusive of Indian, French, African, and Spanish ancestry. The pattern is illustrated graphically in figure 12.1 and described further below.

Among the sixty Creole respondents, 87 percent identified themselves as Creole, 63 percent as French, 57 percent as African American, and 55 percent as Native American. These data in and of themselves challenge the notion of racial and cultural identities as unitary constructs and reveal the inadequacy of instruments and methodologies that are premised on these inherently limiting notions. The use of such instruments inevitably perpetuates disparities in the treatment of mixed-race peoples such as Creoles by limiting their recognition as distinct multiethnic populations and thus rendering them invisible.

Additional results of the survey speak to the complexity and pervasiveness of mixed-race identity within the Creole population and, in particular, the widespread inclusion of Native American identity within the Creole population, as demonstrated in figure 12.2.

As illustrated, 85 percent of the survey respondents endorsed the belief that one does *not* have to be 100 percent Native American to identify as Indian, and 40 percent endorsed the belief that Creoles should be considered Native Americans. Contributing further evidence of the complexity of the identification process, 75 percent thought that Creoles should be identified only as Creole, whereas

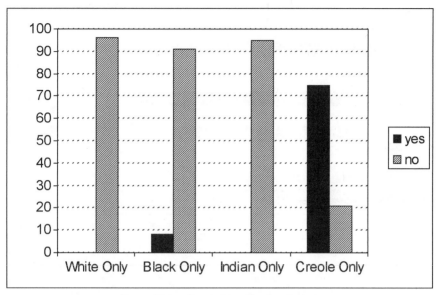

Figure 12.1.   Creole Identification Patterns.
Source: One hundred surveys distributed nationally in the United States and collected by the author from
   August 2001 to October 2001. Margin of error: +/– 3. Response rate: 60 percent.

82 percent thought that individual Creoles with Native American
ancestry should be able to identify as both Creole and Native American, and that the U.S. government should recognize individual
Creoles with Native American ancestry. None of the respondents
believed that Creoles should be identified as white or Native American only. Seven percent of respondents did not respond to the five
questions just reported on respecting the interrelationship of Creole
and Native American identities.

Figures 12.1 and 12.2 graphically depict the results of the survey and represent current trends in Creole thinking about the role
and contributions of American Indian culture to Creole identity,
addressing the controversial questions of whether Creoles should
be legally recognized as an American Indian community and/or
should be identified as a discrete category on the 2010 U.S. federal
census.

These findings suggest a complex pattern of ethnic identity
among the contemporary generation of Creoles living within and
outside of Louisiana. Internal group definitions of what it means to
be Creole are overwhelmingly inclusive of Native American identity.

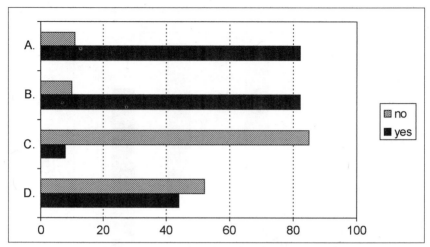

Figure 12.2.   Creole-Indian Identification Patterns.
A. *Should individual Creoles with Native American ancestry be recognized by the U.S. government as Native and Creole?*
B. *Should individual Creoles with Native American ancestry be able to identify as Creole and Native American?*
C. *Do you have to be 100 percent Native American to identify as Native American?*
D. *Should Creoles be considered Native American?*

Source: One hundred surveys distributed nationally in the United States and collected by the author from August 2001 to October 2001. Margin of error: +/– 3. Response rate: 60 percent.

Furthermore, the findings reveal that, while Creoles are inclined to identify most heavily with their French roots, most also see themselves as equally Indian and African. The results demonstrate that the Creole connection to Indian identity is equal in strength to the Creole connection to African identity, though the former connection has been rendered invisible to the outside world and has been largely ignored in other studies of this community.

Individual and Group Interviews

The quantitative survey described above was supplemented by a series of individual and group interviews with Creoles across the continental United States. Data from the interviews further support and substantiate the reported survey findings and add important historical and contextual details about Creole life and identity from an intimate personal perspective.

From July 2001 through May 2004, I conducted one-on-one and small group interviews with a total of thirty-five Creole individuals at conferences in New Orleans, Los Angeles, and Las Vegas. Participants were recruited by selective sampling through staff members at the LCHC, through random selection at conferences, and through snowball methods where individuals were either referred directly or were contacted by the investigator because a previous participant had referred them. All interviews were structured or semistructured and ranged in duration from thirty minutes to two hours. All participants signed informed consent forms that explained the study, its voluntary nature, and its use for my dissertation as well as my intentions for future publication. No compensation was offered for participation in the interviews.

The average age of the interview respondents was thirty-nine years. Of the thirty-five individuals who consented to and participated in interviews, sixteen were men and nineteen were women. Group interviews were mixed according to gender and age and were usually semistructured and more conversational in nature than were the individual interviews. Everyone was asked the same eighteen questions, with spontaneous follow-up questions posed to help clarify individual and group responses to these initial questions. Individual interviews followed the same format as group interviews but had a less open-ended flavor because they involved a two-way dialogue instead of a group discussion. Some group discussions and interviews actually took place during shared meals or after religious services or familial events such as family reunions. All interviews were conducted with the principal investigator in the role of interviewer and were recorded using both audiotapes and handwritten notes. The tapes were then transcribed and analyzed to assess variables and patterns specific to the study's scope.

The following comments of one interview participant summarize the frequent concerns expressed by respondents about the chronic invisibility of the Creole community, attributed in part by this participant to the conceptual and methodological biases of prior researchers:

Part of it is the anthropologists' sort of colonialism that spawned anthropology in the first place. It's where you're always looking for the pristine people . . . people who have their culture. It's the old Boazian thing about finding a whole culture intact. See [John] Swanton wasn't interested in mixed families at all. He was looking for "real" Indians. Like there's a letter, you might run across it, he went below Azeel [*sic*] and he said, "I heard there were some Indians there and I went . . . but when I got there, there were just a bunch of Choctaws mixed with Black." There's a lot of races in those swamps there. I'm sure he was blind to it. But they were never interviewed. There was a linguist, who was married to Mary Haas. He was working on the Chitimacha and she was working on the Tunica and they found a Black man who spoke Chitimacha, what I hate is he probably also spoke Mobilian, but they didn't know that, but he did become one of their Chitimacha informants. But he's one of the few people who they talked to about Blacks and Indians. Nobody much talked to Mexican/mixed people. (French/Indian Respondent, 2001)

These comments speak directly to the issue of Indian-Creole relationships in the state of Louisiana. The reference to "anthropological colonialism" calls into question the tendency of early twentieth-century anthropologists to overemphasize "full blood" or "authentic" Indian culture while ignoring important aspects of Indian cultural participation and linguistic preservation in multigenerational mixed-race contexts. John Swanton, a Smithsonian anthropologist renowned for his studies of many Indian tribes in Mississippi and the lower South, failed to analyze or even document mixed Indian cultural and linguistic practices in his research in Louisiana. This glaring omission is a clear example of the ways in which methodological biases and limited understanding of the realities of identity among members of mixed racial and cultural groups drastically constrain the contents and utility of research data obtained in this area.

Rethinking Region and the Boundaries of White-Black Identity

Seeking a better life for themselves and their children, many Creole families moved out of Louisiana during the 1940s, '50s, and early '60s, with the intention of continuing to express and maintain their Creole culture in their new communities. The following comments by one Creole mother whose family participated in this emigration speak to the challenges faced by Creole migrant children who attended schools in the north during this period.

> I remember when we moved from Louisiana. My sons had a really hard time, especially my younger son who was darker than his brother, but still very light. In school kids didn't know what to think of him, or where he fit in. He always tried to go with the black kids, but to them he just wasn't "black enough" and there were days when he would get beat up just because he looked, in their words, "so white." To this day he still tries very hard to be acknowledged and accepted by the black community. He always asked me, "Mom . . . why do I have to look like this? Why do I have to be Creole?" And I told him that this was his culture and that yes, he was different, but that he should be proud of who he is and not try to change. (Personal Communication/Interview, Creole Family Convention, Los Angeles, 2002)

As demonstrated in this first-person account, once settled in their new locations, Creole families found little external recognition of their cultural and racial identities. In fact, to their surprise, they found it was difficult for non-Creoles outside of Louisiana to understand what a Creole was, due largely to the social silence surrounding mixed-race identities and their total obfuscation under federal and state law and public policy, which essentially conceptualized race as a binary phenomenon.

Many Creole parents were deeply influenced by these views, which were predominant throughout the segregated South and within the political climate of the 1950s and early 1960s. Some explicitly taught their children to relinquish deliberately their identity as Creoles, as recounted by the following respondent whose parents instructed him and his siblings to choose between black and white, the only options given during those days; what seemed to some to be a third option, "colored," included Indian but was ultimately interpreted to mean black.

> In the late 1950s my daddy went up to San Francisco. I think he drove his Cadillac. He went to meet my uncles who had already relocated to the Santa Rosa area. When my daddy came back he and my mama sat us kids down and explained that we were no longer Creoles. If anyone asked when we moved up North we

should say that we were French Canadians. They then turned on the television and told us to watch the Imitation of Life. This was a movie about the tragic life of a mulatta girl who looked white and hated having a black mother. She had a terrible life and her mother died eventually leaving the young woman all alone. Then our parents told us to choose what we wanted to be. I always knew we were Indian and White, but I chose black. Of my five siblings I always said we had 2 1/2 blacks and 2 1/2 whites. We all identified differently and we didn't know much about our Indian people anymore, so we all made our choices I guess, but it's a new generation for my kids who can make their own decisions now. (Creole Respondent, 2001)

Despite the difficulties they faced in the absence of external validation and with the pressure to conform to inaccurate and self-limiting concepts of racial identity, Creole families found various covert ways to preserve their identities and culture. One of the most significant of these areas involved the religious beliefs they passed along to Creole youth. In a 1989 study of the religious lives of Creoles in their twenties, Sr. Frances Jerome Woods reported that 64 percent of the Creole youth surveyed believed that their religion strengthened their family lives; while only 30 percent of other Catholic youth concurred with the statement. Sixty percent of the young Creoles attended Mass at least once weekly, compared to 23 percent of their non-Creole counterparts. Although young Creoles took exception to Church norms on abortion and nonmarital status, they did so in equal measure with the other Catholic young people studied. Eighty-two percent of the Creole youth endorsed a belief in life after death and in heaven as a paradise of pleasure and delights.

These findings demonstrate the significant role played by Catholicism in the lives of many Creole youth and illustrate the extent to which older generations succeeded in conveying traditional values to them. The results are particularly noteworthy, Sr. Woods observes, because the respondents were "an age when establishing themselves as responsible adults might mean distancing themselves from the ways of their parents and older generations" (Metoyer 1991). Sr. Woods's analysis obliquely raises the question of whether the processes of individual identity formation and psychological individuation differ qualitatively between youth of publicly unacknowledged mixed racial/cultural backgrounds and youth who grow up in publicly recognized, socially sanctioned, homogeneous cultural communities.

Woods's (1989) study indicates that religion was an essential variable in the reconstruction and rearticulation of a Creole community that was less concerned with "authenticity" and "racial purity" and more frequently focused on the importance of culture and family traditions and rituals. Despite the problems surrounding white-black identity construction, Creoles were able to maintain a sense of their culture outside of Louisiana through the many social clubs and activities they created and sponsored in urban areas such as Los Angeles, San Francisco, Oakland, Chicago, Detroit, and New York (Creole Respondent, Los Angeles Conference). The broad sweep of these locations through all corners of the United States demonstrates that success of the Creole population in preserving its rich traditions and beliefs despite regional differences. For example, California-born Creole Janet Colson recounts that boucheries (butcheries) in urban and rural areas of California replicated exactly the experience of their Louisiana counterparts (Fontenot 2002). As the account in which Colson is quoted concludes, "Creoles carry their traditions with them."

These traditions reflect some of the subtle and not-so-subtle ways in which Creoles differ culturally from other ethnic groups with whom they have been associated, despite obvious similarities with the various groups that have contributed to their complex ethnic identity. Some Creole customs are American Indian, while others directly resemble French, African, or Spanish traditions. Fontenot, also quoted in the *Creole Chronicles* (2002: 6), remarks on the presence of social clubs in the Lake Charles area, where families and friends from small south Louisiana communities who had moved to Lake Charles for jobs and economic stability "came together for various events to keep the closeness of the Creole communities they left."

Creoles outside of the rural country parish towns of the southwest and northwest have created a form of transstate travel, much like immigrants from Europe, Asia, Africa, and Latin America who have formed transnational communities from which they leave and return to their places of origin, transplanting their cultures in new locations and regions of the world. When these transstate travelers leave home to visit Creoles within the diaspora, they—much like their transnational counterparts—are inclined to bring things from "home." The reunion traditions of one Creole family are described vividly in the following passage:

> Family reunions in the LeDee family are not limited to Louisiana. Many of Elva's relatives moved to California. Her father, her mother's oldest brother, and a cousin moved to San Francisco. Her mother's sister lives in Anaheim, and many other relatives are spread through the San Francisco, Los Angeles County, and Orange County areas. When Elva visits, it becomes a reunion. Cousins arrive for special meals and spread out across the floor. Elva brings food items that are not found in California and prepares special dishes that remind the relatives of home. She brings Camelia brand red beans, sausage, boudin, tasso, and a particular favorite, gingerbread. The foods are handled with care. She freezes the meat items and packs them in a suitcase for the trip. The forty gingerbreads are layered between her clothes in another suitcase. Relatives encourage Elva to bring plenty of food with the admonition that they will furnish her with all of the clothes that she needs while visiting! (Fontenot 2002: 33)

Family reunion events of this type are a regular feature of Creole life and were commented on repeatedly by the participants who were interviewed in this study as a primary means through which the community continued to assert itself as a distinct entity despite geographical separation.

Many Creoles of Color have retained various aspects of their complex ethnic ancestries not only through religion and reunions, but through other cultural practices such as food, dance, music, and storytelling. Creoles have worked to move beyond the limited and limiting construction of blackness and whiteness that has plagued most of the mixed-race colonial and postcolonial population of the Americas. Creoles have not only been organizing locally, nationally, and internationally, but their everyday cultural rituals reflect an embedded sense of their indigenous ancestries. In one particular example, Creoles continue to preserve their American Indian heritage through the filé making process (a process and ingredient learned from the Choctaw), which involves the use of sassafras leaves to make filé for gumbos and other traditional Creole foods.

Cane River Creole, historian, and preservationist, Michael Moran, better known as "Mickey," is very knowledgeable about filé making. In 1982, Moran's uncle taught him how to process and gather the leaves to make the filé. Certain traditions as well as techniques are involved with making filé. Many people still hold to the older tradition of picking the leaves on August 15, a holy day in the Catholic religion and a day on which most people in past years did not have to work. However, another guideline is to pick after the first full moon in August. The leaves must be dried in a dark place, but only one who has learned the art can tell when the leaves are dry enough. The leaves are ground and sifted to produce a fine powder. The resulting filé is stored either in jars or in the freezer for use as a seasoning and thickener in gumbos and other Creole dishes. About four years ago, Moran taught the process to his boys, Michael and Matthew, then eleven and eight years old, respectively. Having handed this part of Creole culture and tradition down to his sons, filé making has become a family affair at the Moran household (Moran 1998: 28).

Creole community activities and organizations across the country have grown to attract attention at the national level, bringing the general public to a greater recognition of the diversity of the Creole people's history and contemporary existence. Consider for example the following excerpt from a Creole Society publication:

> A special stamp hand cancellation was scheduled to be issued January 20–23 in honor of French Creole Migration according to Sherrell Bozeman, manager of Post Office Operations in Alexandria. A special presentation of the cancellation to the community is to be held at the St. Augustine Catholic Church in Melrose on Saturday, January 20. The Melrose Post Office is one of two postal stations honoring "Creole Heritage Day." The other postal location will be the Baldwin Hill's Crenshaw Plaza Station in Los Angeles California, where the Creole link happened in the mid 1940s when the first wave of Creoles migrated from Louisiana to California. The Louisiana hand cancellation will feature maps of Louisiana and France in honor of the 230th anniversary of the French Creole Migration of Claude Thomas Pierre Metoyer from France to the new world (Louisiana) in 1766. (Moran 1998)

Working to preserve their heritage and to connect with the larger Creole community has been an enormous task, but organizations like the LCHC, along with *Bayou Talk*, St. Augustine's Historical Society, and the Louisiana Folk Life Office have been instrumental in sustaining the current Creole Movement and articulating the ancestral and cultural connections among Creoles and Indians. In 2000, these organizations brought forth a very important presentation at Creole Heritage Day that focused precisely on the Native-Creole connection.

> Regional Folklorist Dr. Dayna Lee will present a paper "Native American Ancestry in the Cane River Community," and Professor of anthropology, Dr. H. F. "Pete" Gregory, curator of the Williamson Museum as NSU, will provide an exhibit on the Caddos and the Creoles. (Colson 2000)

The growth of public attention and the specific inclusion of American Indian aspects of Creole culture reinforce the group's refusal to participate in its own reduction to the classifications of black and white. Rather, Creoles acknowledge and celebrate the vibrant components of a hybrid culture, instead of conforming to a monoracial identity. The community's struggle to move beyond the binary social construction of Creole identity as black-white is often exacerbated by the lack of clarity found in historic records. Lapses and omissions in the historical record more often than not represent the vision and preferences of the dominant culture and represent a challenge even for Creole-initiated genealogical research. For example, the Creole Family History Convention in Los Angeles, California, in 2002 gathered a series of important resources to help Creoles conducting genealogy research to identify their Spanish and American Indian ancestors, with two workshops focusing on the Indian and Spanish influences within Creole culture, a database of family surnames, and a newly established central location for Creole family research. Staff members note that, even in this inclusive context, the dimensions of Indian identity may be difficult to document because they have been unrecorded or obscured in the records from churches and other institutional sources.

> To the best of my knowledge, we have not been able to determine, like what tribe or anything, but I grew up, like I think a lot of people did, under the belief that there were Native Americans within our family. And one of my uncles, who married my father's sister, I knew that he was the descendant of Native Americans, just by the look. But I didn't know that his grandmother, yeah his grandmother, was a sister to my great-grandmother. I didn't know this. So we descended from that same people. I didn't know that

until after I started doing research because I always figured that this was a name that married into our family, and come to find out, we were descendants to that family. . . . Oh definitely, because I cannot really say how, like a definite path that a person would take. Now one thing I can say, that I found last summer (myself personally) some of the church records and some of the census records that indicate a person as Native American in one census, may be labeled something else in the next census. So the other thing is that, in the church records, the baptismal records, they might keep a separate record of slaves or Indians (I found that a record of slaves, those people were actually Indian). So the only thing I could say is that when you're researching your heritage, is that you need to look at everything. If it says that this is a group of white people, do not rule out that your family may not [actually] be Indian. Or if it says slaves, do not rule out that they might not be within that group [Indian]. (Creole Respondent, 2001)

Creole people, like members of other multiethnic populations with Indian ancestry, are often unsure of their exact tribal connection to indigenous groups of North America. Often, parents and grandparents pass down cultural traditions that they identify only as "Creole" because they themselves do not know for sure the identities of the individual tribes that contributed to these practices, or they know that society would not allow them to fully embrace these identities as "legitimate."

On the other hand, the current Creole ethnic resurgence movement continues to confront what has been characterized as an "overemphasis" on black aspects of Creole identity. Many Creoles I spoke with who identified closely with their African American roots spoke of simultaneously feeling pressured to deny the other aspects of their identities. One Creole woman from southeast Texas remarked, "I identify as Black because that's what they say I am, and I don't have a problem with that, but why should I *only* be Black when that's the smallest part of my ethnic background?" (Creole Respondent, 2001). Another woman's comments suggest that many Creoles use the term "Creole" deliberately to reject such reductionism and embrace all of the many ethnicities that contribute to their overall identity.

I think that that part of the culture [Indian] should be recognized. The thing that I always think about, because I've always been asked this question, or it has been said about the center or society or whatever, is "Why don't you wanna recognize your Black heritage?" Its like we're purposefully not recognizing our Black heritage, which is [somewhat] true. How can you say, "Well, I'm gonna recognize the Black heritage today, but tomorrow we'll be Native American?" I think that part of what everyone should recognize is that all of the culture is captured by the center name, "Creole." It's just like, I had this one analogy that I always said I was gonna put on my website, talking about making a chocolate chip cookie. You end up with a chocolate chip cookie, but you don't just go and talk about the flour that went in there! It's a mixture. And what you're looking at is the end product, and there's no reason why I'm gonna just sit here and talk about the flour or the chocolate chips. So to me it's the same analogy; I'm gonna talk about that end product, and how it affects me and what made it—I'll give the ingredients but there's no reason why I'll just talk about one. (Creole Respondent, 2001)

The "chocolate chip cookie" metaphor expressed by this interviewee provides a rich analogy through which we can speak about the American Indian aspects of Creole culture. Over time, American Indians have been like the flour of that cookie. No one ever says, "Mmm, that flour sure made this a great cookie!" The flour is a hidden but necessary ingredient, without which the cookie itself would not exist. However, based on cultural conventions and social expectations, many people tend instead to focus on the chocolate chips or the sugar, just as many prefer to focus on the black or white elements of the Creole mixture. Unlike cookies, however, Creoles are complex human subjects, and the negotiation of their distinct, many-faceted identities during the last century has been a complex, multigenerational process.

Discussion

The data collected in this study clearly reveal a pattern of personal and community self-identification as both Creole and Native American among the majority of the research participants. Quantitative and qualitative analyses demonstrate that Creoles regard the cultural contributions from all aspects of their identity as being equal. As the rates of interracial mixing continue in Native American communities across the United States, the potential significance of the work presented here is enormous. Among other things, this research strongly supports the movement to ensure the rights of indigenous communities to self-identify, using culture and not biological determinism to define themselves over time.

In order to fully understand these data, we need more research and in-depth theoretical analyses to address how cultural formation among multigenerational mixed-race populations can challenge binary racial classification and community authentication practices. These are just some of the many questions that can be raised only after we have done the work explicitly to recognize the social and cultural realities of racially and culturally mixed communities. With such outcomes in mind, the present study and others like it have the potential to lead to entirely new lines of inquiry within ethnic and Native American studies.

Creoles in the United States today are, for the first time, able to make visible their Native identities—in their own words and voices—as fluid, intact, and socially meaningful. As a multigenerational mixed-race Native community, Creoles are one of the last indigenous populations on the continent to be discussed in the scholarly literature because so much of the shared history between Creoles and Indians has been lost, hidden, destroyed, or unrecorded. To fully understand the operations of cultural formation, we need to cultivate a greater understanding of the politics and potential social effects of black-Indian relations, sociocultural disparities, identity perception, and community sustainability.

There is also a need for further research into the possibilities of alliances between ethnic and cultural communities throughout the Americas who are similar to Creoles in their Latin (French and/ or Spanish), Indian, European, and African ancestries, who have similarly melded Catholicism with Indian and African cultures and who have articulated post- and decolonial identities that can include Indian in the naming of their existence as Creole, Puerto Rican, Cuban, Dominican, Jamaican, Haitian . . . at once multiethnic and indigenous.

Throughout the Americas, indigenous communities are struggling to gain respect and acknowledgment of their sovereign political, social, economic, legal, and regional status as nations. Rearticulating a specific place for multiethnic indigenous communities that have historically been racialized along the lines of non-Native, biracial,

European-African only communities can offer a new framework for understanding the importance of culture and cultural formation in shaping ethnicity and, perhaps more importantly, for linking ethnicity with individual and group identity: what people *do*, *feel*, and *articulate* as their own lived experience.

Creoles offer us an important lesson about the futility of reducing race and ethnicity to biology, law, and even history. Creoles of Color demonstrate that to understand the full complexity of identity as a sociological phenomenon, scholars must link all of these different variables and, in the process, withstand any temptation to simplify or reduce identity to a dichotomy of extremes. Creoles in the twenty-first century continue to fight to move outside of the extreme binary conceptualization of race and, in the process, to assert a clearly Creole identity that encompasses everything that we are—American Indian, French, Spanish, and African—as indigenous, multiethnic, and diasporic peoples.

One of my concerns in designing and implementing this study was the notion that identities can become mutually exclusive when they apply to multiracial people. There are many examples of local Creole people who work to preserve their identities even as these change over time. It is important to note that no ethnic group goes without changing in terms of dress, language, appearance, and even in terms of culture. So then, at what point in history does one stop being Indian if this has been a part of one's identity? Does a multiracial identity necessarily negate or privilege one aspect of identity over others?

Racial formation theory assumes that racial identities are socially constructed and therefore change over time as societal forces exert pressure on these constructs to become different or remain the same. The one-drop rule (the notion that one drop of black blood is all it takes to "qualify" a person as black) is one example of the way in which racial formation theory demonstrates the significance of race, while ignoring culture in influencing and even interrupting the notion that society completely controls individual ethnic identity options. The Creole case in fact provides evidence to the contrary. Despite the outside pressures and society's long history of racializing them as "black," Creoles have successfully maintained a coherent, albeit multifaceted, identity that they themselves experience and authenticate. The formation of Creole organizations throughout the twentieth century provides evidence of the ways in which groups organize themselves around community and culture rather than physical appearance alone. Cultural formation, in contradistinction to racial formation, provides for a deeper analysis of the ways in which cultural practice, cultural symbols, and signs of cultural identity contradict the static definitions of race against which they argue. More specifically, to understand fully how race and racism are products of ideology, one must understand the ways in which cultural formations disarticulate the "logics" of intact racial identities. To question the notions of race, racism, and the hegemony of racial projects, we must be able to produce an alternative framework for arguing against a racial agenda.

The Creoles provide us with an instructive case in point. Creoles distinguish themselves not so much by biology as by culture. In the interviews conducted in California, Texas, and Louisiana during the two-part study reported herein, most of the participants discussed the meaning of their Creole identities in the context of social gatherings, music, dances or La-La's, church ceremonies, and ethnic festivals. As their responses demonstrate, although racial identity or biology is the initial factor that gives a group its identity, it is not what maintains. Creoles have preserved their distinct identity not simply because of biology (which the research indicates has changed over time) but mostly through their vibrant, shared culture. Similarly, American Indians are defined today within most tribal communities not simply by biology, but also by community participation, geography, awareness of cultural traditions, and shared history. Thus, degree of blood—though still used in some parts of the country today as a determinant of race—is often far less significant to Indians and Creoles than cultural identification and participation.

Additionally, the interviews reported here argue against the historical view of Creoles as "performing" race. Instead, a constructionist or social interactionist model is of far greater utility in helping to clarify the many ways in which Creoles have been forced by their surroundings and by the hegemonic construction of racial identity to shift from a collective group identity as Creole to individual identification with specific points within the continuum of French, Indian, Spanish, and African ancestry. Larger structural state apparatuses have compelled Creole migrants to deny the complexity of their ethnic and cultural distinctiveness and have instead

Figure 12.3. Left to right: Author's father, Kenneth, and uncle Charles.

ensured the perpetuation of an inaccurate and overly simplified view of Creole people by not offering a "Creole" category on any census forms.

Conclusion

This essay reports on the results of a two-part ethnographic study of ethnic self-identification and regional invisibility of Creoles in

Figure 12.4.   Left to right: Author's aunts Greta, Joelle, and Karen.

the United States, conducted from 2001 to 2004, which incorporated both a survey and a series of in-depth individual and group
interviews with members of the contemporary Creole community
across forty U.S. cities. The study adds to the handful of research
reports that are based on data obtained primarily from Creole people themselves and represents the first research ever performed in
the United States on Creole-Indian identity formation.

The survey reveals that Creoles from around the United States
believe strongly that their group should first and foremost be
identified legally and socially as Creole. Additionally, it is clear
from the results of the survey that to the members of the Creole
community themselves, the Native American aspects of the group's
ancestry are equally as important a part of the group's heritage as
are the African and European aspects. Finally, data obtained from

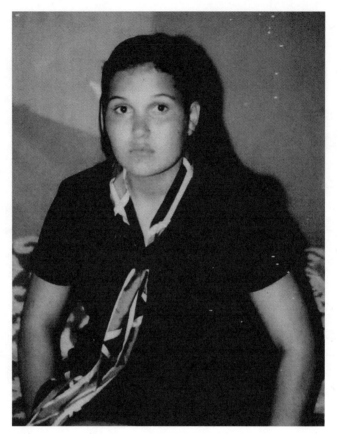

Figure 12.5.   Author's aunt/godmother Joelle Jolivette-Gonzalez.

both the survey and from a parallel set of in-depth semistructured interviews reveal that, despite various pressures to deny their multiracial ancestry, Creoles have maintained a continuous connection to the self-proclaimed identity as Creole and to their original homeland in Louisiana, expressing, celebrating, and perpetuating this identity through the practice of rituals related to religion and the Catholic Church, cooking and family social gatherings and celebrations throughout the Creole diaspora.

The implications of this work are profound and promising in their potential contribution to the body of literature on ethnic studies and American Indian identity, demonstrating, for example, the limitations of the black-white paradigm of racial identity in the

United States. The reported findings also illustrate how the ethnic civil rights movements in the United States during the 1960s paradoxically led to particular constraints on the ability of Creoles to assert their own multiethnic identity as a community of French, American Indian, African, and Spanish descent. Despite the confluence of legal, political, and social factors that have denied its existence or sought to eradicate it, the identity of the Creole community continues to remain strong and vibrant—if largely unrecognized by outsiders—on the continent today and, therefore, has much to teach us about the ability of communities to, in the words of anthropologist James Clifford, "articulate themselves."

The survey and interview data reported here indicate that a clear majority of Creole respondents across the United States believe that Creoles should be able to identify as "multiracial," Creole and American Indian, French, and Spanish at the same time. As the elders in the community informed me over the course of my research, no individual identity within the larger Creole makeup is more valuable than any other. At the conferences I attended in Los Angeles, New Orleans, and Las Vegas, I participated in workshops on the Spanish, French, American Indian, Caribbean, and Haitian influence on the Louisiana Creole alongside a wide range of participants of clearly different phenotypes—ranging in appearance from European to American Indian, to Latino and African American. In this space, the unifying element was culture, a complex amalgamation of Louisiana ancestry, family names, and personal involvement in Creole cultural activities such as masses, dances, food, and historical celebrations. No matter what you looked liked, if you could participate, you were family: You were Creole.

Note

I would like to acknowledge the support of my dissertation chair, John Brown Childs, at the University of California, Santa Cruz; Tomas Almaguer, my faculty mentor at San Francisco State University; Barbara Ustanko for her excellent editorial assistance; and the Ford Foundation Postdoctoral Fellowship Award Program, which allowed me to secure important release time from my teaching duties to complete this research project, which was in part based on research conducted for my dissertation at UC Santa Cruz.

References

Adams, Jolene M., and Fusilier, Freida M. "He, La-Bas!: A History of Louisiana Cajun and Zydeco Music in California." 2002. Available at www.cal.net/louisianasue/ehlabas.htm.

Brasseaux, Carl A., Keith P. Fontenot, and Calude F. Oubre. *Creoles of Color in the Bayou Country*. Jackson: University of Mississippi Press, 1996.

Clifford, James. "Indigenous Articulations." Address delivered at the conference "Native Pacific Cultural Studies at the Edge," Center for Cultural Studies, University of California, Santa Cruz, February 11–12, 2000.

Colson, Janet. *Creole Heritage Day Program Booklet*. Natchitoches, LA: Northwestern State University, 2000.

Deloria, Vine. *Custer Died for Your Sins: An Indian Manifesto*. Norman: University of Oklahoma Press, 1988.

Delphin, Terrel. *The Creole Struggle and Resurrection: Our Story as Told by Creoles*. Natchitoches, LA: Northwestern State University Library, 1995.

Dominguez, Virginia. *White By Definition: Social Classification in Creole Louisiana*. New Brunswick, NJ: Rutgers University Press, 1997 [1987].

Dormon, James H. "Ethnicity and Identity: Creoles of Color in Twentieth Century South Louisiana." In *Creoles of Color of the Gulf South*, edited by James H. Dormon. Knoxville: University of Tennessee Press, 1996.

Fontenot, Michael. "Boucheries and Other Celebrations: Lake Charles Louisiana." In *The Creole Chronicles*, vol. 2. Natchitoches, LA: Northwestern State University, 2002.

Gehman, Mary. *The Free People of Color of New Orleans*. New Orleans: Margaret Media, 1994.

Hall, Gwendolyn Midlo. *Africans in Colonial Louisiana: The Development of Afro-Creole Culture in the Eighteenth Century*. Baton Rouge: Louisiana State University Press, 1992.

Kein, Sybil. *Creole: The History and Legacy of Louisiana's Free People of Color*. Baton Rouge: Louisiana State University, 2000.

Martin, Joan. "Placage and the Louisiana Gens De Couleur Libre: How Race and Sex Defined the Lifestyles of Free Women of Color." In *Creole: The History and Legacy of Louisiana's Free People of Color*, edited by Sybil Kein. Baton Rouge: Louisiana State University Press, 2000.

Metoyer, Louis. "Sr. Woods Update." In *Bayou Talk Newspaper*, vol. 5, no. 11. Moreno Valley and West Covina: JO VAL, 1991.

Mills, Gary. *The Forgotten People: Cane River's Creoles of Color*. Baton Rouge: Louisiana State University, 1977.

Moran, Mickey. "The Filé Making Process." In *Creole Heritage Day Program Booklet*. Natchitoches, LA: Northwestern State University, 1998.

Ravare, Malinda. "Louisiana to California." In "The Natchitoches NSU Folk Festival." Natchitoches, LA: Northwestern State University.

Saint Augustine Historical Society. "Program Brochure." Natchitoches, LA: Author, 1998.

Saint Augustine Historical Society. "Creole Heritage Day Celebrations: The Past 7 Years, 1994–2000." Natchitoches, LA: Author, 2000.

Woods, Sr. Frances Jerome. *Value Retention Among Young Creoles: Attitudes and Commitment of Contemporary Youth.* Mellen Studies in Sociology, vol. 5. Lewiston, NY: Edwin Mellen Press, 1989.

Index

About the Contributors

Norma Alarcón is professor of women's studies, ethnic studies, Spanish, and Portuguese at the University of California, Berkeley. She is the author of a book on the Mexican writer Rosario Castellanos, *Ninfomanía: El Discurso de la diferencia en la obra poetica de Rosario Castellanos*, and the author of numerous essays on Chicana writers and on critical theory. Professor Alarcón is the editor and publisher of Third Woman Press as well as the coeditor of the book *Between Woman and Nation: Nationalisms, Transnational Feminisms, and the State*.

Paula Gunn Allen, Laguna, Sioux, and Lebanese, is a poet, novelist, and critic. She was born in Cubero, New Mexico, the middle of five children, having two older sisters and two younger brothers. She grew up on the Laguna Pueblo, beneath Mt. Taylor. She spent a postdoctoral year at UCLA and then moved to the University of California, Berkeley, where she held a postdoctoral fellowship from the Ford Foundation and the National Research Council to study the oral tradition elements in Native American literature. She has also been an associate fellow at the Stanford Humanities Institute. She has taught at Fort Lewis College, Durango, Colorado; the College of San Mateo; San Diego State University; San Francisco State University, where she was the director of the Native American Studies Program; the University of New Mexico, Albuquerque; and the University of California, Berkeley, where she was professor of Native American/ethnic studies. She retired from her position as professor of English/creative writing/American Indian studies at the University of California, Los

Angeles, in 1999. Paula received the Lifetime Achievement Award from the *Native Writer's Circle* of the Americas in 2001. She received the American Book Award from the Before Columbus Foundation in 1990 for *Spider Woman's Granddaughters: Traditional Tales and Contemporary Writing*. She also received the Susan Koppelman Award from the Popular American Culture Associations and the Native American Prize for Literature. Paula is the author of numerous books and compilations of poetry and prose, and her work has been included in more than twenty edited anthologies on American Indian women, identity, history, the oral tradition, and literature.

Carolyn Dunn of Muscogee, Seminole, Cherokee, Creole, and Cajun ancestry is a doctoral student at the University of Southern California in the American Studies and Ethnicity Program. She completed her B.A. in speech communication in 1986 from Humboldt State University and received an M.A. in American Indian studies from the University of California, Los Angeles, in 1992. In the intervening years she has been an educator, poet, writer, and composer. Her work has appeared in the anthologies: *The Color of Resistance, Reinventing the Enemy's Language, Through the Eye of the Deer*, and Kenneth Lincoln's *Sing with the Heart of A Bear: Fusions of Native and American Poetry*. The author of many articles that have appeared in journals in the United States, Canada, and Germany, she is the coeditor of *Through the Eye of the Deer* (with Carol Comfort) and *Hozho: Walking in Beauty* (with Paula Gunn Allen) and the author of a volume of poetry, *Outfoxing Coyote*. She has taught at Humboldt State University, Four Winds Indian School in Chico, California, and California Polytechnic State University, Pomona. She is a member of the all-woman Native drum group the Mankillers, whose CDs include: *All Woman Northern Drum* and *Comin to Getcha!* She is currently examining cultural production among American Indians in Los Angeles, California.

Troy R. Johnson is a professor of history at California State University, Long Beach. He is an internationally published author and is the author or coauthor of fifteen books and the senior consulting editor for thirty-one books plus one additional book currently under contract. His publications include *Contemporary Native American Political Issues, The Occupation of Alcatraz, American Indian Activ-*

ism: Alcatraz to the Longest Walk, and the recently revised book *Red Power.* Dr. Johnson has published numerous scholarly articles and has spoken at thirty-eight conferences across the United States.

Andrew Jolivétte (editor) is an assistant professor in the American Indian Studies Department and also teaches in the Ethnic Studies Program at San Francisco State University. He recently completed a Ford Foundation Postdoctoral Fellowship through the National Academy of Sciences and the National Research Council. Professor Jolivétte is a mixed-race studies specialist with a particular interest in Black-Indian relations, Creole studies, and mixed-race health disparities. He is currently in the process of writing a manuscript based on his doctoral dissertation, *Creole Community Formation: Exploring Mixed Race Native American Identity.* He received Ph.D. and master's degrees in sociology from the University of California, Santa Cruz. He is the board president of Speak Out Speakers and Artist Agency in Emeryville, California, and also serves on the board of FUSION, a summer program for mixed-heritage youth in the San Francisco Bay Area. He is a Creole of Opelousa, Choctaw, Atakapa, French, African, and Spanish descent.

Philip Klasky is a lecturer in the American Indian Studies Department at San Francisco State University, where he teaches courses in American Indian religion and philosophy. He is also an adjunct faculty member at New College of San Francisco and at Merritt College. His areas of research interest include cultural preservation and revitalization; language preservation; ethnographic audio and video recording of indigenous story, song, and language; and the study of toxic colonialism. He is actively involved in the community as director of the Storyscape Project at the Cultural Conservancy of San Francisco, as a board member of the Institute for Deep Ecology, and as a board member of the Escalante Wilderness Project. Professor Klasky's recent publications and research presentations include: "Unbroken Circle: The Xavante Indians of Brazil Reach Out in Their Struggle to Protect Their Traditional Culture and Lands" (*Earth Island Journal*), "Storyscapes: Living Songs in Native Lands" (*ReVision Magazine*), and "Preserving Culture through Ethnographic Recording" (presentation through the Cultural Conservancy of San Francisco).

Winona LaDuke is an Anishinaabeg (Ojibwe) enrolled member of the Mississippi Band of Anishinaabeg and is the mother of three children. LaDuke is the program director of Honor the Earth and founding director of White Earth Land Recovery Project. Leading Honor the Earth, she provides vision and leadership for the organization's Re-granting Program and its Strategic Initiatives. In addition, she has worked for two decades on the land issues of the White Earth Reservation, including litigation over land rights in the 1980s. In 1989, she received the Reebok Human Rights Award, with which in part she began the White Earth Land Recovery Project. In 1994, LaDuke was nominated by *Time Magazine* as one of America's fifty most promising leaders under forty years of age, and she has also been awarded the Thomas Merton Award in 1996, the Ann Bancroft Award, *Ms. Magazine* Woman of the Year Award (with the Indigo Girls in 1997), the Global Green Award, and numerous other honors. A graduate of Harvard and Antioch Universities, she has written extensively on Native American and environmental issues. Her books include: *Last Standing Woman* (fiction), *All Our Relations* (nonfiction), *In the Sugarbush* (children's), and *The Winona LaDuke Reader*.

Melissa K. Nelson, assistant professor of American Indian studies at San Francisco State University is an enrolled member of the Turtle Mountain Band of Chippewa Indians and is of mixed-blood heritage: Chippewa (Ojibwe) and French (Métis) from her mother and Norwegian from her father. She is also a writer, researcher, and activist who focuses on the protection and restoration of indigenous lands and cultures. Professor Nelson is the executive director and president of The Cultural Conservancy, an indigenous rights nonprofit organization based in San Francisco. Melissa has published articles and essays in various journals such as *Orion Magazine, Restoration & Management Notes, ReVision Journal, Abya Yala News, The Trumpeter,* and *Turtle Mountain Times.* In 1999 one of her essays, "Becoming Métis," was published in the anthology, *At Home on the Earth: Becoming Native to Our Place.* The same essay will also appear in *The Colors of Nature.* Professor Nelson's other publications include: "Contemporary Native American Responses to Environmental Threats in Indian Country," coauthored with Dr. Tirso Gonzales in *Indigenous Traditions and Ecology: The Interbeing of Cosmology and Community,* and "Constructing a Confluence," for the Terra Nova anthology *Writing On Water.* Melissa currently serves on the board of directors of the Golden Gate Biosphere Reserve and the Interfaith Center at the Presidio. She is also on the editorial board of *Revision*, a journal of consciousness and transformation. She is a former board member of Earth Island Institute and the Collective Heritage Institute and served as an associate producer for their annual Bioneers Conference from 1999–2001. In 1994 she was awarded scholarships from the American Indian Graduate Center and the Native American Scholarship Fund and in 1999 and 2002 she received Switzer Environmental Leadership Awards for her work with The Cultural Conservancy.

Kim Shuck is an artist, poet, and mathematician. Her artwork has shown in galleries and museums nationally and internationally and is often based in both her various cultural backgrounds and her interest in math. Her poetry has been published in anthologies and literary magazines in the United States and Canada. She is a member of the board of directors for the California Poets in the Schools. As a former professor at San Francisco State in the American Indian Studies Department, her courses included American Indian Science, American Indian Oral Literature, and American Indian Art. While at SFSU she was the chair of the Jaques Johnet Scholarship Committee and the faculty adviser for the National Association of Black Accountants Inc. She was also the faculty adviser to SKINS (Student Kouncil of Intertribal Nations). Kim is a member of the Wordcraft Circle of Native Writers and recently completed a book of poetry.

Sara C. Sutler-Cohen received her Ph.D. from the Department of Sociology at the University of California, Santa Cruz. Her dissertation is an ethnographic study of neoshamanism in Northern California. Through long interviews and participant observation, she has constructed a study that moves away from the critiques of the commodification of indigenous spiritualities and toward an attempt at a politically and culturally critical understanding of what has been called "White Shamanism." She is the current editor for *Native Realities*, the online journal for Wordcraft Circle of Native Writers and Storytellers, and the area chair for Native/Indigenous studies for the Popular Culture and American Culture Associations' Southwest/ Texas Annual Regional Conferences. She lives with her ten-year-old son and her partner in Portland, Oregon.